HUMAN RIGHTS AND THE NEW WORLD ORDER:

UNIVERSALITY, ACCEPTABILITY AND HUMAN DIVERSITY

HUMAN RIGHTS AND THE NEW WORLD ORDER:

UNIVERSALITY, ACCEPTABILITY AND HUMAN DIVERSITY

BAMIDELE A. OJO

NOVA SCIENCE PUBLISHERS, INC.
Commack, NY

Creative Design: Gavin Aghamore

Editorial Production: Susan Boriotti

Assistant Vice President/Art Director: Maria Ester Hawrys

Office Manager: Annette Hellinger

Graphics: Frank Grucci

Manuscript Coordinator: Phyllis Gaynor

Book Production: Joanne Bennette, Michelle Keller, Ludmila Kwartiroff, Christine Mathosian, Joanne Metal, Tammy Sauter and Tatiana Shohov

Circulation: Iyatunde Abdullah, Sharon Britton, and Cathy DeGregory

Library of Congress Cataloging-in-Publication Data
available upon request

ISBN 1-56072-438-2

Copyright © 1997 by Nova Science Publishers, Inc.
6080 Jericho Turnpike, Suite 207
Commack, New York 11725
Tele. 516-499-3103   Fax 516-499-3146
E-Mail: Novascience@earthlink.net

Printed in the United States of America

DEDICATION

I dedicate this exercise to my children: Bamidele Adesegun Ojo, Jr. and Miss Kofoworola I. Ojo-Adesegun and to the children all over the world, for whom we must prepare the future, first, by guaranteeing necessary and fundamental rights and second by implementing these rights so that they (children) can live their lives to the fullest.

**Bamidele A. Ojo
Assistant Professor of Political Science
School of Political & International Studies.
Fairleigh Dickinson University.
Teaneck. New Jersey. United States of America.
B.Sc(Social Sc)Hons. Political Science
M.Sc International Relations[Ife, Nigeria].
DELF (Cavilam, University of Clemont Ferand, France)
Diploma in French (Ife, Nigeria)
M. Phil/DEA Etudes Africaine(African studies)
Bordeaux, France.
LLM International Law (Nottingham, England)
DIHL (International Humanitarian Law,
Wegimont, (ICRC) Belgium)
Ph.D Political Science(Bordeaux, France)
Associate Member, International Institute for
Humanitarian Law, San Remo, Italia.

CONTENTS

FORWARD

"Human Rights and the New World Order: Universality, Acceptability and Human Diversity" is an examination of the variant nature of the human rights concept, in a attempt to identify its relationship to the questions of universal acceptability and human diversity. The goal is also to determine the possible impact of contemporary international order on the interpretations and implementation of international human right regimes. Given the diverse socio-political and economic conditions within which these regimes are to be implemented, the tradition has been to predicate human rights applications on superficial and inconsequential but politically conditioned rational and this has been made possible by the lack of effective enforcement procedures and mechanisms.

Upon identification of the limits of implementation, the emphasis is on the need for effective restructuring of the United Nations and the need to recognize the universal nature of human rights. Recognizing that these rights are inherent in humans by virtue of their existence and that these rights should therefore be assumable by all humans wherever they may be and should be enforced, if not by locally responsible agents then by regionally responsible agents or surely by internationally responsible agents. Without humans and their assumable rights, these agents, these structures - such as States and governments, would not exist or possess the rights to function in the first place.

- Bamidele A. Ojo

ACKNOWLEDGEMENTS

I am grateful to Prof. D.J. Harris, for the assistance and advise he offered, both as my Head of Department and Director of Thesis, at the Department of Law, University of Nottingham, England. He did all he could to make this exercise a success. I also want to thank Dr. N.D. White, Mr. I.R. Edmund, and Mr. McCoubrey for their assistance and timely suggestions.

My special gratitude to the Department of Law, University of Nottingham, England for their awards: Montefiore (1988) and J.C. Smith (1989).

And to my family, Mosunmola [Wife], Junior, and Kofo'[Children], I appreciate their understanding and cooperation.

RIGHT IS RIGHT:

CONCEPTUALIZING HUMAN RIGHTS

The concept of human rights has evolved over the ages. This evolution has not only rendered the concept more controversial but difficult to apply universally, as an instrument for maintaining human dignity and integrity. For centuries now, it has been the centre of political thinking and aspiration. Not only has it been demanded as a protection against tyranny but as an assurance against inhuman treatments and unjust punishments within political entities. The concept has also transcended its normal environment within national states into internationalized concern for the protection of human freedom.

The most important organ of its internationalization in this century, was forty-eight years old on December 10, 1996. This is a reference to the Universal Declaration of Human Rights adopted in 1948 by the United Nations General Assembly. Its aim was to recognise human rights situation in any part of the world, as a legitimate matter of international concern. This objective can be said to have been achieved because[and since then], human rights concern has gained outstanding international recognition and subsequent instruments which later emerged as a result of it, not only went further in setting the necessary standard but laid the ground for further declarations and conventions in specialized fields such as elimination of racial discrimination, slavery, genocide, etc. But it is by far easier to set standards through drafted conventions and declarations than actual implementations of the aspired objectives therein. It is in this regard that the controversy surrounding the human rights concept requires further attention.

Many intellectual exercises and theories attributed the problems of implementation (and of the realization of its global application) of human rights to the different interpretations given to it, at different times and in different parts of the world. As a result of which there has been a call for a systematic speculation of the subject and a definition of its desirable goal, in order to redress the distortion which inhibit the proper application of human rights, even forty-eight years after it has been universally declared.

This exercise is not an attempt to achieve this lofty goal, but a means through which the end required can be justified and probably realized. The purpose of this exercise is two-fold.

First, it is an *effort* at analyzing the evolution of the human rights concept, while taking into cognizance its increasing variants, which has been attributed to the evolution in "time and space." This objective is to be carried out through objective and critical examination of the human rights literature, both in historical and analytical (but theoretical) perspectives, in an effort to identify the universal nature of human right .

The second objective is a critical evaluation of the growing contradiction which the evolutionary nature of the concept has generated. This part is directly related to the first, because it will indicate the implication of the evolution other wise referred to (and its consequence) and if possible, identify what the future trend might be.

This book is divided into two parts, with the first dealing with the examination of the evolution of the concept- human rights, while focusing on the period since the 1948 declaration. In this part, there is an examination of the strands of debates that have characterized the evolutionary nature of the concept, given the socio-political and economic changes since the second world war.

Part I is divided into six chapters, of which Chapter 1 gives a general presentation of the subject and the different approaches used in the study of human rights. Chapter 2 examines the concept of Rights. In this Chapter, rights is examined as a duty; as a claim; as entitlement; as interest or utility and as choice or benefits. In Chapter 3, we examines the concept of human rights as different or related to other rights, such as moral, natural, legal or political rights.

While in chapter 4, we undertook a study and critical examination the universal declaration of human rights and in chapter 5, the trends and evolution of the concept during the cold war and after. In chapter 6, we examine human rights development in the developing areas of the world while using Africa as a case study.

The Second part of this book is focused on the human rights in the post cold war environment. This part examine the changing socio-political environment in the world and its impact on the human rights application while taking cognisance of the inherent problem of human diversity. In chapter 7, we examine the new world order while chapter 8 focus extensively on the constraints existing in the present international climate such as questions of domestic jurisdiction, sanction, etc. Chapters 9 and 10 examines the question of human diversity and the future of universal human rights application respectively.

This analysis is not in itself exhaustive and neither does it claim to be so, the main objective as earlier stated, is to create a synthesis of the varying dimension of the concept of human rights and the practicality of its application in a new world environment. This is a revised version of the LLM International Law thesis submitted for the degree in 1989 at the Department of Law, University of Nottingham, England.

PART I: CONCEPTUALIZING HUMAN RIGHTS

Chapter 1

APPROACHES: ANALYSING HUMAN RIGHTS

The increased concern for the treatment of fellow human being is a positive development in all aspect of human life. The evolution of such a concern in the form of legal rules underscore the importance of such a development. Since legal rules are the reflection of social standards, as demonstrated by the French Revolution, the law itself becomes an expression of the general will, which results in the change in social attitudes towards human problems. This is more apparent with the abolition of slavery, which is a product of the positiveness of legal rules. The same trend, led to the prohibition of other forms of uncivilised human behaviour, in the early part of this century, such as, genocide, arbitrary arrest, detention without trial, political execution, torture and racial discrimination(among others). However, the mere fact that some of these uncivilised behaviours continue to exist is not an indication that attempts to prevent them by international actions are inconsequential. That they continue to exist may in fact underline our lack of conviction and effective implementation of these measures that were put in place to eradicate them. Our preoccupation should be in effective implementation of measures already in place.

One of the common reasons given for the ineffectiveness in implementing human rights regimes has been attributed to the absence of a clear definitional approach. Human rights varies in context, origin and it means a different thing to each individual or a group of individuals, in a given place and time. One of the effort of this exercise is to identify the various dimensions of the human rights concept by presenting a synthesis with the aim of identifying its basic principles.

Contrary to opinion that little effort has been made in an attempt to create a "comprehensive map of the totality of human rights[1]", the concept has in fact, generated heated academic exercises in recent years and the inherent confusion otherwise referred to by many, is simply a result of the multi-variant nature of the concept itself. The study of human rights has been approached in different ways, among which are: the natural law approach, the historical approach, the positivist approach, the Marxist or communist approach, and the social science approach.

It must be re-emphasised at this point, that this study is not going to engage in polemics for or against any particular approach (or theory) to the study of human rights, neither is it going to identify (by supporting) any of the theories or conceptions (or approaches) but rather, to analyze them in order to define the limit of the discourse and help in creating a universally acceptable and clear intellectual map of the concept.

The Natural Law approach, is based on the premise that there are natural laws both theological and metaphysical which confer certain particular rights upon individuals. These rights derives their authority either in "divine will or in specified meta-physical absolutes.[2]" This approach contributed to the discourse, by emphasising the realities of naked power and that of a higher authority, which is asserted to require the protection of individual rights.

Its focus has been a common identification with the whole of humanity, which emphasises a common human nature with comparable rights and equality for all. However, its conception of authority has been given as its principal inadequacy[3]" because authority is conceived in terms of divine will or metaphysical absolutes which gave little or no room for comprehensive and selective inquiry about empirical processes which is indispensable to the management of the variables that affect decisions. But it gave human right that universal aura, that is applicable to all human being anywhere in the world.

The historical approach on the other hand conceives human rights in terms of factual demand of community members for participation in different value processes. It define "authority" in the finite perspective - the "living law" of the members of a particular community. It emphasize the fact that the human right demanded and protected within any given community is a function of the many cultural and environmental variables unique to that community[4]. The major contribution of this approach has been its provision of a framework of theory for the realistic and contextual examination of particular situation in which the degree of protection of human rights is under challenge or at stake.

It also stressed the importance of the time and space dimension of human rights problem and afforded the knowledge of trends in degrees of realization through time and in different communities. It presented also a modest, preliminary approximation of the causal analysis that is a characteristic of social sciences. However, its principal defect has been the almost total immersion of inquiry within an undifferentiated community[5]. It has been criticised for not distinguishing the demands of individual human beings from the demands made in the name of the aggregate of community members. This approach also reinforce, the importance of particularistic nature of each society.

The third approach is the positivist approach which advanced the position that the most important measure of human rights is to be found in the authoritative enactment of a system of law sustained by organized community coercion[6].

Its emphasis is upon "the institutions of modern state, and it is inspired by and inflated with exaggerated notions of sovereignty and that only nation-states, and not individual human beings, are appropriate subjects, of international law[7]."

The contribution of this approach has been its recognition of the importance of bringing organized community coercion and the state's established processes of authoritative decisions to bear upon the protection of human rights. It has enhanced the protection of many particular rights and strengthened explicit concern for more comprehensive means of fulfilment, by focusing upon deprivations in concrete situations and by stressing the importance of structures and procedures, as well as prescription at the implementation phase.

The Marxist (communist) approach projects human rights as the inevitable realization of a meta-physical determinism that proceeds in harmony with the laws of dialectical materialism[8].

The world social process is conceived as a continuing class struggle generated by the concentrated control of production in a comparatively few hands. In this situation [in a society], in which the bourgeois class monopolises the means of production, human rights are alleged to be little more than illusions. It is only in a society where the means of production is publicly owned, can human rights become a reality. Its contribution therefore has been its initial intense concern for human dignity.

However, there are inadequacies, especially concerning its persistent theme that human rights appertain not to the individual person but to the collectivity (and especially to that collectivity known as the nation-state). Given the recent decline of the Soviet empire and the limitations placed on human rights on behalf of the state and the good of the public, communism as it apparently turned out, sustained the domination of the power elite at the expense of the people.

The Social Sciences approach builds upon the theories and techniques of modern science to enhance our knowledge of the factors that affect failures and successes in the protection of human rights[9]. It proposes relevant theories and techniques for investigating causes and effect in relation to human rights in the larger context of the social process. It gave prominence to theoretical models and empirical procedures by which data can be gathered and processed to supplement the more traditional philosophical and historical inquiries[10].

These approaches are complementary to one another and in many cases underscore the variant nature of the human rights concept itself.

Chapter 2

WHAT IS A RIGHT?

The origin of the concept- human right, can be dated to ancient Egyptian, Greek, Roman, Babylonian, Hebrew or oriental civilizations. It has also been influenced by political thinkers, prominent among which is John Locke. He saw it as a fundamental right, to property - that the body is the original property and the sources of the civic and political rights. He was a great influence on both the American independence and the French declaration of Rights. Neither can we ignore the contribution of John Stuart Mill on natural rights and individual rights. And in 1845, long before the "Communist Manifesto," in his publication "The Holy Family," Karl Marx acknowledged the existence of human rights while attacking the notion of natural rights and emphasising that most of the political and civic rights are meaningless unless one has an economic and educational foundation adequate to take advantage of them[1].

To begin our discussion, we might as well try answering the simple question, what is a right ?

A: RIGHT?

From the Lockean concept of the state of nature in which the individual is in a "state of perfect freedom to order their actions and dispose of their possession and persons as they think fit, within the bound of the law of nature, without asking leave or depending upon the will of any other sect.[2]" The bounds of the law of nature requires that "no one ought to harm another in his life, health, liberty, or possession.[3]"

This means that in a state of nature, an individual may himself enforce his rights, defend himself, exact compensation and punish (or at least try his best to do so) and others may join with him in his defence, at his call[4]. Certain distinctive features shows that the concept of right as grounded as it may be in history still demonstrates some considerable overlapping.

According to the right based theories, interest of each individual should be considered one at a time, thereby leading to individualistic consideration theories of rights which makes it more complex. Rights has been distinctly defined and categorized into three in terms of its forces. These includes;(a) That "Rights" is nothing but a particular important interest, which is assigned a greater weight than ordinary interest and therefore counts for more in utilitarian or other welfarist calculations[5]; (b) That the interest's protected by rights are given lexical priority over other interests[6]. These interests are to be protected and promoted to the greatest extent possible before other interests are even taken into consideration. According to Waldron, this makes rights absolute against consideration of mere utility, but leaves open the possibility of what Robert Nozick called "a utilitarianism of rights" - which involves maximizing fulfilment, minimizing violations when they conflict inter se[7].; (c) That rights are understood not as specially or lexically weighted interests, but as the basis of strict constraining requirements on actions. The function of a right is to exclude certain forms of behaviour involving other people from intentional consideration. Rights, in other words, define the boundaries of practical deliberation - your having the right not to be tortured makes it wrong even to contemplate torturing you[8].

Apart from the above distinctions of the forces of rights, the relation between natural rights and natural law is another aspect of the "rights talk." Both of which have a long history from the Stoics and Roman jurists to the Atlantic Charter and Roosevelt's four freedoms[9]. This relationship is of course manifested in the form of natural equality of men manifested with both the French and

American Revolutions. However, some clarifications are necessary about the evolution of this relationship. There are many aspects of human well being and the commitments, projects and actions that are apt for realizing them are innumerable even for an individual contemplating his own life-plan. But when the complexities of collaboration, coordination and mutual restraint involved in the pursuit of the common good are contemplated, we are faced with inescapable choices between rationally eligible but competing possible institutions, policies, programmes, laws and decisions.

The strength of rights talk, according to John Finis[10] is that, "carefully employed, it can express precisely the various aspects of a decision involving more than one person, indicating just what is and what is not required of each person concerned and just when and how one of those persons can affect those requirements." To Finis, the conclusory force of ascription of rights, is the source of its potential for confusing the rational process of investigating and determining what justice requires in a given context.

The dynamics, otherwise stated above, is manifested in the forty-eight years old Universal Declaration of Human Rights. The declaration is in keeping with the tradition of natural law in its differentiation between rights accruing to all men everywhere and those which are identified as separately enacted in the positive law of each state. According to B. Harold Levy[11] the declaration which was to be only a formulation of "standards of achievement, combines the natural law emphasis on universal ideals with the positive-law emphasis on potential enforcement. To him, the combined emphasis is expressed through the proclaimed expectation that the rights will eventually receive appropriate national and international measures of implementation." These characteristics and the nature of the Universal declaration, will be examined in the chapter 4.

B: RIGHT AS DUTY

Another dimension of the rights talk involves its relation with duty. Under the classical natural law theory, the person with a "right" is also under duty[12]. Rights and duties are therefore linked in the one person. These rights are not absolute, but neither can duties and social consequences of acts be ignored[13]. Pope John illustrated such reciprocity between rights and duties as:

"The rights of every man to life is correlative with the duty to preserve it; his right to a decent standard of living with the duty of living it becomingly; and his right to investigate the truth freely, with the duty of pursuing it ever more completely and profoundly...[14]"

This relationship with duty demonstrate the immunity concept and the classical viewpoint expressed in recent human rights declarations. For example, the Universal Declaration of Human Rights identify duties of the individual to the community as correlative to "the free and full development of his personality[15]." On the contrary, the European Social Charter did not refer to either duty or responsibility[16]. To Hohfeld, the clue to the concept "Right" when used as a synonym for claims lies in the correlative "duty" (These concepts give rise in their own turn to different legal doctrines)[17].

The denial or the assertion of a right will be upheld only if it furthers the common good. Such rights (or equivalent of claims - see below) are not absolute, and ordinate in an ideal, nor in a social compact. On the other hand, a right in the absolute sense is an immunity, which is a restriction on governmental power and is not socially conditioned. According to Rousseau, law is conceived as a universal objective determined through the general will (in other words, rights are not a summation of private wills - because private wills are directed towards preferences) while general will is an objective identifying what is best for all and, although cumulative through individual assertion, is universal in content. But Locke on the contrary, mixes the two contradictory concepts - immunities and the common good (which is derived from claims).

C: RIGHTS AS CLAIMS

Another dimension in the understanding of the concept of rights is seeing it in terms of claims which is the wants, desires and aspirations people have and expresses. These claims which people make, may be on behalf of others or themselves. It may involve claims which are supported by or in accord with some objective standard - or some general theory - whether those of a code of morality or ethical theory, or those of a political system or political theory, or those of a legal system which are usually and aptly called rights[18].

Claims that are recognized within a code of morality or an ethical theory, is therefore moral or ethical rights. While claims recognized in various ways in a political system or theory is political rights. It is therefore possible for a particular claim to acquire triple characters of moral, political and legal rights. An example in modern England is the claim to physical integrity and not to be injured by others. Another aspect in this complex relationship, is the possibility of a particular claim to rank only as a moral right, in a particular society i.e. in the former Soviet Union -the claim by political dissidents of freedom to criticize the government-[19].

The analysis of legal rights can be taken even further as did F.E. Dowrick, into rights stricto-sensu, legal freedoms, legal powers and legal immunities.

This bring us to the concept of natural rights, in which, the normative precept that "no one ought to arm another in his life or health" yielded for Locke and others, the particular proposition that every individual person had a 'natural right' to life and to physical integrity. i.e. individuals' claims to life and physical integrity are in accord with these general ethical norms. In the context of ethical or political arguments therefore, these are immediately understood as universal precepts for a moral standard for political systems. The doctrine of 'natural rights' in effect argues that these precepts should be implemented in all societies at all time.

D: RIGHT AS ENTITLEMENT

Another interesting dimension to the debate is the equation of right to entitlement[20]. To say that one has a right to something, is to say that, that person is entitled to it. For example, entitlement to an old-age pension, to vote, to free medical treatment or to ones own opinion. It is even more convenient, to distinguish between rights of action and rights of recipience[21]. The right of action emphasizes what one is entitled to do while the right of recipience, emphasizes what one is entitled to expect (to receive or more generally, how one is entitled to be treated). However, the right to freedom cuts across the distinction made above because it is both a right of action and a right of recipience. It is the most general right of action whereby one is entitled to do anything which is not expressly forbidden. But it is also a right of recipience - that is one is entitled not to be coerced or interfered with, so long as one does not do what is expressly forbidden.

This notion identify the fact that, every substantial right entails a correlative obligation, upon other people, i.e. the case of rights or recipience. If I am entitled to receive something, there must be someone else, or perhaps some official or agency with an obligation to provide me with it. One might be tempted to conclude that the relationship between rights and obligation must be symmetrical - not only does every right entail correlative obligations, every obligation entails correlative rights.

One can therefore infer that rights are essentially social in character - which is true of both legal and customary rights. One can have them only as a member of a particular community with its own legal system and body of customs. It is also true of the rights which go with membership of voluntary associations, such as clubs, trade unions, universities - such rights are quasi legal in character.

E: RIGHTS AS "INTEREST, UTILITY AND INDIVIDUATED"

Another conception of rights is that which involves its relation or equation with interest, utility and individuated political aim. These political aims are considered as not being subordinate to the conception of "aggregate collective good[22]", or the "general interest[23]" or "general utility[24]." To Finnis, such a conception of rights would give reason for concluding that the reference 'general welfare' in Article 29 of the Universal Declaration of Human Rights is inept. He indicated also that "in defining or explaining rights, we must not make reference to concepts which are incoherent or senseless for example conceptions of "aggregate collective good" are incoherent, "save in limited" technical context - and the ongoing life of a human community is not a limited technical context[25].

F: RIGHTS AS CHOICE AND BENEFITS

The equation of rights to choice and benefits is also another aspect of the rights debate." Harts' presentation of the choice theory is no accident because it was associated with a more general thesis that, the right to liberty was both fundamental to and presupposed by all other claims about individual rights[26]. According To Jeremy Waldron, "we should note that, although benefits and interest theories are more accommodating to the socio-economic rights (and to the rights of children and animal too)[27], still in any such theory, not every interest is going to be regarded as the basis of a right but only whose protection or advancement is taken to be a matter of special concern."

G: RIGHT$_1$, RIGHT$_2$, RIGHT$_3$, RIGHT$_4$... RIGHT$_X$

Before ending our general examination of the rights family, the analysis of Honfeld (in its demonstration of realism in law [this is also well demonstrated in L. E. Allen[28]]) in which he uses rights to denote a wide variety of legal relations[29], is worth mentioning. Honfeld stipulates rights as follows:

Right$_1$ right (in strict sense)
Right$_2$ privilege
Right$_3$ power
Right$_4$ immunity

According to him, right in the strict sense of a legally enforceable claim should refer to the correlative of 'duty' (as earlier enumerated). That is, if X has a right against Y that he shall stay off the former's land, the correlative (and equivalent) is that Y is under a duty toward X to stay off the place. Also right could be used to indicate a privilege to do something = Right$_2$. Honfeld in this wise, classified right in terms of "privilege" which refers to what a person was permitted to do as far as some other person was concerned:

" [W]hereas X has a right or claim that Y the other man should stay off the land, he himself has the privilege of entering on the land; or in equivalent words, X does not have a duty to stay off. The privilege of entering is the relation of a duty to stay off."

Just like in Right$_1$ "Right", Right$_2$ "privilege" refers to a three term relationship between two persons and an action - namely the privilege holder, the other party and an act of the privilege holder.

"To say that X has a (legal) privilege, to do P, as far as Y is concerned is the same as to say that it is permissible for P to be done as far as Y is concerned by Y and that the legal system will not enforce any attempt through litigation by Y to prevent X from doing P."

Right$_3$ = Power, is different from the two above (Right$_1$, Right$_2$) because it refers to a two term relationship ($_{1,2,3,4}$)which demonstrated what Honfeld said about 'right', 'privilege' 'power' and 'immunity'.

From the foregoings, the following observations could be made: That, if the end product of every political association is the preservation of the natural rights of man, "then governments must be set up and constitutions structured in such a way that it becomes impossible for individual rights to be pushed aside for the sake of the private interests of those in power or even in pursuit of other social goals and aspirations[31]."

From the above analysis there is an apparent attempt by philosophers and jurists to be much more precise in their use of the concept of a right.(as its relationship logically to duty, obligations and the concept of law had preoccupied ancient thinkers and jurists)[32].

But "rights" has not been immune from evotivist or relativist doubts of moral truth and objectivity in general. According to Waldron, the idea that there might be such things as rights, valid for all peoples in all times and spaces, has often seemed implausible in the face of the wide variety of what we would call "oppressive and inhumane practices that are taken for granted - even expected - in different parts of the world." These difficulties do not impede the right talk but from the analysis so far, it is clear that many theorists simply repudiate "ethical skepticism and moral relativism[33]." To some other theories, meta-ethics do not by themselves entail any view about what can or should be said at the level of moral judgement[34].

Waldron further asserts that:

"Even if it is true, for example, that moral judgements are nothing but expression of attitudes, it does not follow that,   it   is   mistaken   or fallacious to express the attitudes we have, nor does it follow that it is wrong to give vent to an attitude which is categorical and implicitly universal in the scope of its application: To say that a statement like "All men have the right to equal liberty" is just an expression of emotion is not to make any recommendation about the desirability or otherwise of expressing emotions of this sort."[35]

However, it must be emphasized that epistemological difficulties have made a difference to the way people have written and thought about rights.

In ethics, if meta-ethical realism is untenable, then rationally resolvable disputes become possible only between those who share certain fundamental values or principles in common. This is important in the area of the right talk as in other areas, since philosophers need to identify clearly the deep assumptions on which their theories depend. For example, if two different theories of rights rest on a common commitment to the importance of individual liberty, there is a principle, no reason why any detailed disagreements between them should not be rationally resolved. But if the theories, on the contrary, are based on different fundamental values, i.e. one is based on liberty and the other on a commitment to equality - then, to the extent that there is incompatibility between these deep commitments, there may be no way of resolving their

surface disagreements. This meta-ethical problem, according to Waldron, has driven modern exponents of
individual rights to stake a much greater interest in the deep values and principles that underlie the details of the particular rights that they proclaim[36].

Another characteristic that can be deduced from the "right talk" is the fact that some people have attempted to relate the idea of rights to a particular aspect of moral personality - the active practical and assertive side of human life as opposed to the passive, effective, or even pathological side. Rights have been seen as a basis of protection not for all human interests but for those specifically related to choice, self-determination, agency and independence - However, the approach concerning socio-economic rights, has been criticised as a debasement of the language of rights[37].

One can therefore conclude that, an individual is considered as having a right to some opportunity or resources or liberty, if it counts in favor of a political decision and that the decision is likely to advance or protect the state of affairs in which he enjoys the right. Rights are instrumental in the sense that they function as means to an end. When men claim as rights certain freedoms and protections they do so because these are felt to be necessary to secure their integrity as human beings and to assure them the opportunity to exercise and develop their human capacities. The primary locus of right might be said to lie in the sense of injustice. Rights have their origin in the effort to address what is experienced as an undeserved harm, that is, as wrong. Philosophers such as Hobbes, Locke and Rousseau and of course, political thinkers like many leaders of the American and the French Revolutions, each had a clear, if not always identical conception of the right (that is conditions and guarantee) that must be assured to men if they were to live with any security and decency.

However, the different clauses of the Bill of Rights, like the due process and equal protection clause must be understood as appealing to moral concepts rather than laying down particular concepts - One might tend to support some writers and philosophers, who reject the idea that citizens have rights apart from what the law was -"nonsense on stilts" -,i.e., does the acknowledgement of the right to free speech for example, include the right to participate in "nuisance demonstrations?

Chapter 3

HUMAN RIGHTS

(A) HUMAN RIGHTS

Human rights fall into the family of rights, which is such a large family. There are legal rights, moral rights and natural rights thereby giving room to considerable overlapping, because a right that is legal may also be a moral right, though not all are. A right that is moral is often not legal, though some also are. And a right that is taken to be natural is often considered as moral, while some are legal, though some are thought to be beyond the scope of law[1].

There are lots of skepticism about whether human rights really exist and whether they can be universal[2]. Taking cognizance of pragmatic analysis that human rights are universal and inalienable and that these rights are grounded in the nature of man as a rational creature, capable of freedom and suffering[3], the idea of human rights as expressed in the universal declaration of human rights, is an ideal standard which every human community should try to reach. The universality is clearly affirmed in Article 2 of the Declaration of 1948.

The question of universality is examined in the second part of this book although distinguishing between the various rights i.e. natural rights, moral rights, legal rights and political rights, is important and it does not reduce the importance of their universal applicability as human rights. But it is evident from contemporary analysis that, to speak of natural rights requires a conception of "nature" and to speak of moral rights demands for a conceptualization of "morality[4]". Speaking of legal and political rights also requires both the conceptions of "law" and a "political state[5]". To conceptualize "human" - that is, what it means to be human[6],is to speak of human rights.

The concept- human rights, is not just ancient history but was also "the dominant form of political theory in Christian Europe since the fourth century[7]". It is also a relative *new*comer to the scene in the sense that its emergence in the 18th century French declaration of the rights of man seems to involve a basic philosophical humanism in which man becomes the touchstone of reason, if reason is taken to be the essence of man[7]. In spite of this, human rights is distinct from the other forms of rights.

Human Rights is distinguished from legal and political rights because it is seen as belonging to a person because he is a human being, while legal and political rights require at least that one should be a member of a given legal or political community - that is one's possession of such a right is completely contingent upon such membership. But the possession of human rights is not contingent upon membership in a legal-political community (and the rules of that community). According to Blackstone, the possession of human rights is generally seen as the ground for making claims both against nations and across national and legal-political boundaries.

It is also the case with "natural" rights. Natural rights theorists see the very "raison d'être" for legal structures and political government as the protection of natural rights. The state is conceived as the guarantor of these rights and if it fails in its functions, it loses its legitimacy. It is in this realm that the two doctrines - natural and human rights - seem to be identical[8].
And it is this role of legitimizing state that will be the discussed in the second part of this book dealing while with the questions of universality and acceptability.

However, Dowrick does not see the human rights this way[9]. He believes that since the middle of the 20th Century, human rights, influenced by the terminology of the universal declaration has been used where earlier exponents of universal ethics such as Locke, Rousseau and the founding fathers of the American constitutions spoke of "natural rights." These concepts are not synonymous because the change in adjective indicates a change in content because most exponents of human rights in the middle and late 20th century were referring to a vastly wider range of rights for individuals than partisans of "natural rights" had in mind in former centuries.
human rights, therefore, is a modern version of natural rights, and to analyze what is distinctively human rights is not only of theoretical importance but also increasingly of practical and social importance - since the concept is being employed with growing frequency in the area of claims advanced by

both morality and law. Just like in rights per se, there is also a relationship between claims and human rights, but in this case, a distinction is made, in the sense that, not every claim is in the full sense, a right[10].

But in the words of J.E.S. Fawcett, "there is a distinction between rights and claims and when we speak of rights, we imply that there is, or ought to be, some means of their enforcement now. But there are countless human needs and human demand which ought to be met but which can be met only in the future, either for material reasons or because they are in conflict with each other and can only be properly met in the resolution of the conflict. These needs and demands are really claims and it is problematic if we try prematurely to treat them as rights.[11]" It is important that we should not underestimate the dialectical relationship between personal claims and human rights because, as Lauterpacht emphasized, "while they (human rights) are bound to be mischievous when conceived as alternatives to changes in the law they are of abiding potency and beneficence as the foundation of its ultimate validity and as a standard of its approximation to justice.

In as much as, in the final analysis, they are an expression of moral claims, they are a powerful lever of legal reform, the moral claims of today are often the legal rights of tomorrow.[12]" In a counter-claim however, Doyle raised the issue of the fact that, human rights are based on the claims of person qua person and that these claims in turn are based on consideration of social injustice and are directed primarily against those with power and authority to mitigate or eliminate social injustice[13]".

Human Rights can be considered not only as a claim made by men for themselves or on behalf of other men taking cognizance of the humanity of man and man as a member of human kind. The essence of the humanity can therefore be guaranteed in the preservation of the well being of human being. However, these aspects of human well being are many which requires a commitments, projects and actions that are apt for realizing these well being are innumerable, even for an individual contemplating only his own life-plan, talk less of contemplating the complexities of collaborations, coordination and mutual restraints, involved in the pursuit of the common good, which one is confronted with giving inescapable choices between rationally eligible but competing possible institutions, policies, programmes, laws and decisions.

There is a core of basic rights which is common to all cultures despite their apparently divergent theories and possible implementation strategies and consistent with the natural rights tradition thereby emphasizing the desire to establish universal human rights not in the pursuit of what is common to all cultures but in a production of a list which takes something from all cultures. For example, that "human rights that were properly universal would do something for Islam and for China (and for Africa,) rather than relying on the straight forward conversion of western into universal values[13.2]".

To demonstrate the relationship between nature of states and their tendency toward implementation human rights, Vincent classify the roles of states into: states founded precisely for the purpose of securing for their citizen the human rights that everyone ought to enjoy (i.e. U.S. and France); states, which whatever the reasons for their establishment are coming to terms with expanding international law of human rights (*The Fujii case*) and a situation which has the domestic courts of one state upholding the international law of human rights, that the offense against human rights was committed by a foreigner in his or her own state (i.e. *Filartiga v Pena-lrala*)[*].

The universal declaration of human rights, signed forty-eight years ago on the 10th. of December 1948 has some distinctively striking features and the most surprising of which is its reflection of what is considered as a fundamental antimony in modern philosophy that include the co-existence of the values of liberty and equality. These two values which were proclaimed as companions in the 17th and 18th centuries' political philosophy of Locke and Rousseau, later turned out in modern political and jurist theory in practice to be a major rival(i.e. - the preamble of the declaration as well as its Article 1 proclaim both values).

Articles 3 - 21, relating to life, liberty of the person, conscience, expression and the security of the person and the right to fair trial and the democratic rights to vote and participate in a central government, presuppose the basic values of liberty. While Article 2, the non-discrimination clause and Articles 22 - 27, which declares the economic and social rights depends upon the basic value of equality. One may probably wonder, whether this divergence would not inhibit the effective functioning and application of the declaration. In the 19th Century, J.S. Mill would have given priority to liberty, while Karl Marx would have insisted on the priority of equality.

---

[*] In Richard P. Claude, "The Case of J. Filartiga and the Clinic of Hope", *Human Rights Quarterly*, Vol. 5, (1983) No. 3, p.275-301.

This divergence manifested itself sharply in the working sessions of the UN Commission on Human rights 1947 - 48, in the exchanges between the representatives of the western democracies and the Soviet Union and the eastern European states. There was also the bitter exchanges of the Belgrade Conference in 1977 - 78, the follow up to the Helsinki final act, between the USSR and the U.S.A. are manifestations of this particular problem. This problem also raised its ugly head at the philosophical level.

In the 1970's, John Rawls in *A Theory of Justice* (1972) came out strongly in favour of liberty, albeit 'equal liberty' whereas Ronald Dworking in *Taking Rights Seriously* (1977), argues towards priority for equality, viz the fundamental right to 'equal concern and respect'[14].

Chapter 4

THE UNIVERSAL DECLARATION OF HUMAN RIGHTS

The purpose of the declaration was to define the human rights and fundamental freedoms asserted in the United Nations Charter and to place them before the world as a standard of achievement for all people and all nations[1.] One may be tempted to ask whether the declaration is necessary, when there exist certain provisions already in the charter.

Considering the fact that, human rights obligations set out in the charter were drafted in intentionally vague language and given the human rights provisions in the charter and the various human rights instruments that have been adopted under it, it became clear that the subject of human rights was no longer a matter essentially within the domestic jurisdiction of individual states as it was set out in Article 2(7) of the charter.

But the most important precipitant of the universal declaration is no doubt, the effect of the gross violations of human rights that were committed in and by certain countries during and immediately before the second world war. These atrocities fostered the climate of world opinion which made it possible for the San Francisco Conference to make the promotion of respect for human rights and fundamental freedom "for all without distinction as to race, sex, language, or religion," one of the corner stones of the United Nations[2]. However, it was in Article 68, that the Economic and Social Council was instructed to set up a commission for the promotion of human rights, and this became one of the first acts of the Council[3]. And the Human Rights Commission, under Eleanor Roosevelt's chairmanship, later drafted what became the Universal Declaration.

Amongst the rights proclaimed in the declaration are the rights to: life, liberty, security of person (Article 3), equality before the law (Article 7), privacy (Article 12), marriage and protection of family life (Article 16), property (Article 17), Social Security and the 'realization, through national effort and international cooperation... of the economic social and cultural rights indispensable for' (everyone's dignity and the free development of personality) (Article 22).

It also include the rights to participate in government (Article 21), work, protection against unemployment, favorable remuneration of work (Article 23), rest and leisure (Article 24), a standard of living adequate for... health and well being... (Article 25), education (Article 26), enjoyment of the Arts and a share in the benefits of scientific advancement (Article 27) and 'a social and international order in which the rights and freedoms set forth in this declaration can be fully realized' (Article 28).

This an "human rights manifesto[4]" and an outline of the common good and the various aspects of individual well being in the community which therefore means, that each and everyone's well being in each of its basic aspects must be considered and favoured at all times by those responsible for coordinating the common life. The adoption of the declaration was a milestone in the history of human rights in this century.

It was a great achievement and took on a moral and political authority "not possessed by any other contemporary international instrument, with the exception of the charter itself[5]".

Forty-eight years later, it possesses both moral and political authority and has become an international standard by which the conduct of governments is judged both within and outside the United Nations.

It has inspired a whole lot of treaties (and Conventions) i.e. European Convention for the Protection of Human Rights and Fundamental Freedoms[6]. It is reflected in many national constitutions, international legislations and in decisions of both national and international courts[7].

But the question that readily comes to mind about the declaration, is whether it has any force of law, despite its forty-eight years of existence. There is however the need to emphasize that the declaration does have the quality of law, and because it is not a treaty, it should not be denied this quality. But an understanding of value should be based on the premise that as law, it acquires normative binding from the source of authority from which it emanates. And as an international law it is the will of the international community, which has been expressed traditionally, either by customary rules or indirectly by treaties, which are themselves binding by virtue of the customary rule, pacta sunt servando.

The statue of International Court of Justice added another value, which is "the general principles of law recognized by civilized nations"[8], and therefore the principles set forth in the declaration are "general principles of law." And as Humphrey puts it, those principles would be part of international law by virtue of their recognition by the legal systems of "civilized nations" and not because they are proclaimed by the universal declaration[9].

Moreover, forty-eight years, is quite enough to establish a practice as a custom and as Justice J. Tanaka wrote in his dissenting opinion in *the Continental Shelf cases*, "the speedy tempo of present international life promoted by highly developed communication... has diminished the importance of the time factor and made possible the acceleration of the formation of customary international law. What required a hundred years in former days may now require less than ten years[10]". The time factor here, is even long enough to establish the principles of the Declaration constituting a custom in international law. The point is, if at all the declaration does not have any legal force, it should be regarded as contributing to the creation of international law, for it is considered as the source of both international covenants, such as the Civil and Political Rights and that of Economic, Social and Cultural Rights (and many other international treaties). Also important is its(declaration) relation to the United Nations Charter because it is frequently used as an authentic interpretation of the latter. The declaration also reflects at least a minimum standard which every human community should try to reach. Just as the French declaration of the rights of man and citizens was an amalgam of ethical and political doctrines of 18th century Europe so does(on a wider basis) the rights proclaimed in the universal declaration of human rights relates to an amalgam of ethical doctrines, with rationalistic and theological roots and of various 20th Century political doctrines[11].

But the adoption of such a document is one thing while its implementation in actual societies is another especially when the provisions denotes, a varying degree of contradictions, which cannot be fully implemented[12].

These provisions includes, the right 'to freedom of expression' (Article 19) and the provision that 'no one shall be subjected to arbitrary interference with his privacy... nor to attacks upon his... reputation' (Article 12). And on the other hand, no discrimination on grounds of sex (Article 2) or that 'motherhood... (is) entitled to special care and assistance' (Article 25ii).

There is also the 'right to work' (Article 23) versus the 'right to rest and leisure' (Article 24) . There is the right of everyone to education and the provision that elementary education shall be compulsory (Article 26(i)) which is hard to reconcile with the rights of everyone to 'freedom of thought, conscience and religion' (Article 18) and the 'prior right' of 'parents... to choose the kind of education that shall be given their children' (Article 26(iii)).

Another conflict, is that which concerns the question on whether abortion should be permitted on demand of the pregnant woman: - on behalf of the unborn child - considering the argument that 'everyone has the right to life' (Article 3); on behalf of the mother - considering the provision that 'everyone has the right to freedom of conscience... and to manifest his belief in practice' (Article 18) and that 'no one shall be subjected to arbitrary interference with his privacy, family...' (Article 12).

There is also Article 21 which involves solutions as far apart as a liberal democracy like the United States is from an authoritarian regime, like the former Soviet Union Article 29(iii) authorizes a government to limit the exercise of all the foregoing rights and freedoms to meet the just requirements of 'morality, public order and the general welfare...' and which shall have a priority in a political crisis.

The extent to which these limitations are carried out, is not anything new and is even more complex and wide than the "gulf" that exist between the two societies. The public order limitations are on such rights like, that of liberty (Article 3), security of person (Article 3) and no arbitrary detentions (Article 9), freedom of movement (Article 13) and freedom of peaceful assembly (Article 20).

To grasp the importance of this, consider Article 29 which reads:

1) Everyone has duties to the community in which alone free and full development of his personality is possible.
2) In the exercise of his rights and freedom, everyone shall be subject only to such limitations as are determined by law solely for the purpose of securing due recognition and respect for the rights and freedoms of others and of meeting the just requirements of

morality, public order and the general warfare in a democratic society.

3) These rights and freedom may in no case be exercised contrary to the purposes and principles of the United Nations.

It must be noted that Article 29(2) as limiting clauses also appeared in the European Convention and many other documents. It should be noted also that the limitations in Article 29(2) are said to be on the exercise of the 'rights and freedoms' specified in the declaration. Can one therefore, infer that, the limitations might not be applicable to those articles which do not purport to define a right but instead impose a negative requirement - which could as we have observed, have been expressed as a right but was not.

This no doubt calls for a differentiation in the guiding force of the various articles, as criteria for just laws and decisions. This differentiation goes further, as to how the provisions were coined. Many of the documents of this nature especially, the Universal Declaration and the European Convention use the following forms: -

I.   'Every one has the right to...' and
II. 'No one shall be...'

That is, like in the Universal Declaration; Article 3 - 'Every one has the right to life, liberty and security of person'; Article 4 - 'No one shall be subjected to torture...' etc. Transformation from one coinage to the other can be seen throughout the document (i.e. Article 17(c), or even Article 13(1) etc. and also in the European Convention - Article 5(1) 'Everyone has the right to liberty and security of person' etc.). The point can therefore be made that the Articles coined or expressed in form (ii) - 'No one shall be subjected to...' are intended to be of conclusory force.

Whereas, articles in the form of (i) have guiding force only, as items in a process of national decision-making which cannot reasonably be concluded simply by appealing to any one of these rights - Not forgetting the fact, they are all "fundamental" and "inalienable" and part of everyone's entitlement[13]. The limitation clause (Article 29,(2)) is important and serve some purpose such as the need :

a)   To secure due recognition for the rights and freedom of others

b) To meet the just requirements of morality in a democratic society
c) To meet the just requirements of public order in a democratic society
d) To meet the just requirements of the general welfare in a democratic society

This is one of the many characteristics of the declaration which gives credence to claims by many, that it serve the interest of only western "democratic values" which is imposed on other non- western values in the international system.

The implementation of the declaration ultimately faces the question of its universality

There is also a paradox, for example in the existence of two groups of rights in the Universal declaration, namely, juridical and political rights - Articles 1 to 21, and economic and social rights - Articles 22 to 30. The juridical and political rights presupposes the values and institutions of liberal societies while the economic and social rights those of modern industrial society (note Article 8, 19 and 21 and of course 23, 24 and 25).

The paradox is in terms of the declaration, which professes to be a statement of human rights,- that is the rights of which people have as human beings, irrespective of the particular social and political order under which they happen to live. But then goes on to enumerate a detailed list of rights which presuppose the values and institutions of a certain kind of social and political order, namely liberal, democratic and industrial society.

One can appreciates the problems this declaration and subsequent instruments have faced in their implementation, which has led to developments in the field of human rights, to what is now called "generation of rights." This development especially the "third generation of rights" is an inherent response to inadequacies already referred to - as paradox, in certain socio-cultural environments or units within or between societies. The question is not whether it is justifiable as human rights or not, but that the concept is evolving in direct response to its environment.

There is no such paradox in the European Convention. For example, in its preamble, the signatories, profess allegiance to "a common heritage of political tradition, ideals freedom and the rule of law." But these signatories are governments of liberal democratic states and therefore concerned with protection of human rights (within their states and) between their respective states.

Another evolution out of regionalized approach to maintaining human rights, is the increasing addition to the generations of rights. For example, the African charter confess rights and freedom on individuals and people with corresponding duties. These includes for example: equality before the law, respect for the life and integrity of the persons, right to liberty and security of the persons, right of every individual to have his cause heard, freedom of conscience, the profession and free practice of religion and the right to receive information.

It also include other rights, such as the rights to free association, the right to assemble freely with others, the right to freedom of movement and residence within the borders of the state and the right to participate freely in the government of one's country. These set of rights are classified as civil and political rights or *first generation rights*.

The African charter confers another set of rights: *second generation rights* which include rights such as economic, social and cultural rights. It also include the right to property, right to work under equitable, satisfactory conditioned and receive equal pay for equal work, right to best attainable state of physical and
mental health, the right to education, the right to economic, social and cultural development and duty to the family and the society and the state.

But as important as the above sets of rights and unlike any other international or regional human rights instrument, the African charter goes beyond the above two generations of rights and endows individuals and people with rights which are styled as *third generation of rights*. It includes the right to development, the right of people to dispose of their wealth and national resources and the right to "a general satisfactory environment favorable to... development."

Another important characteristic of the charter, is its emphasis, that all the rights are to be enjoyed at all times. Not even in times of emergency can a state party to it, derogates from its obligation under the charter. And these rights are to be enjoyed without any form of discrimination as clearly stipulated by its article 2. It also emphasized that women in particular are not to be discriminated against.

Despite the fact that all the rights are to be enjoyed at all times, there exist fundamental obstacles such as in: Article 6, which indicates that *"No one may be deprived of his freedom except for reasons and conditions previously laid down by law*;" Article 8 also indicates that "No one may *subject to law and order*, be submitted to measures restricting the exercise of "freedom of conscience and religion."

Interestingly, Article 9 also indicate that "Every individual shall have the right to express and disseminate his *opinion within the law*." In Article 10, "Every individual shall have the right to free association *provided that he abides by the law*. There are more clauses like these, which are dependent upon the laws of the states ratifying the charter, which no doubt, restricts the exercise of these rights.

This is not unique to the African charter, examples can be found in many other instruments in all regions of the world, which continue to create thesis and antithesis in the evolutionary process of the Human Rights concept. Because of the lengthy procedures, the control and influence of the judiciary by the State and its leadership, the personalization of powers coupled with corruption which permeates these societies undermine possible implementation.

Another mitigating factor is the relative poverty of the African population which implies their inability to exhaust the legal procedures. The NGOs are considered the best option available, in communicating atrocities and violations to the commission but they are flagrantly expelled by governments. But the best available hope depend on the on going lies democratization process, which will enhance human rights protection and justice on the continent.

Chapter 5

TRENDS AND EVOLUTION OF RIGHTS

Since the United Nations adoption of the Universal Declaration of human Rights on December 10, 1948, there have been political, economic, social and cultural changes around the World which have individually and collectively impacted on the application, effectiveness, guarantee and the respect for human rights

The aftermath of the declaration has witnesses the coming to effect of many treaties, the most important of which are the European Conventions, the two covenants, the regional charters and the series of conventions on specialized subjects.

Despite all these developments arose out of the need to take cognizance of the different ideological backgrounds, the different historical roots, the contrasting traditions and the diversity of political, economic and social outlook, it must be said that the evolution of human rights since 1948 led to analytical studies which were characterized as "western", "socialist" and "third world" .We can also sub-divide these broad conceptions into regional orientations such as Latin America, or African or Asian.

Care must be taken in categorizing the analysis of human rights into either western, socialist or third world, because of the overlapping and inaccuracy that may develop in the process.

Countries in different parts of the world belong to many of these groups and a strict or rigid geographical identification is therefore difficult to establish. For instance former socialist countries are sometimes categorized as "third world" countries, while some of them are in the western hemisphere. Third world countries also embrace so many countries from Africa, Asia (and notably China) and Latin America.

While it is difficult to establish the existence of a common conceptualization of human rights in the "third world," it is however necessary to identify a common trait,according to H. Gros Espiell, because of " the characteristic, social and economic situations evidences the need for similar approaches to the matter of human rights[1].

Taking cognizance of the impact of underdevelopment, foreign and neo-colonial exploitation, poverty, illness and illiteracy which characterize countries in this category, many of them tend to link human rights to the establishment of new international economic order. There is a characteristic priority to economic developments rather than human rights.

The developing countries of Africa and Asia, with a few exceptions, did not participate in the deliberation resulting in the Universal Declaration, however many took part in the preparation of the Covenants and in the third committee of the General Assembly of 1966, in which they affirmed their priority for economic and social development[2,] which they also re-emphasized during the International Conference of Human Rights in Tehran in 1968[3].

In most of the third world countries is the overdependence on the role of the state and belief in the need for it to take action without hindrance in order to achieve economic and social progress. This particular point runs contrary to the core of the school, which considers it necessary to regulate and control its action, even by international means, in order to guarantee and protect these rights.

The Western perspective recognize the existence of rights and freedoms inherent to man's nature and to his status as an individual which rise above the state and above all political and ideological pluralism and the multi party system. The European Convention for the safeguard of human rights and fundamental freedoms, signed in Rome on November 4th, 1950 established "a system" for the international defense and guarantee of human rights based on a Commission and the European court. It also in 1961 adopted the European economic charter, for the promotion of necessary respect for social and economic rights.

This western regional operation emphasized the possibility of associating local and international systems for the protection of human rights today. In Latin America evolved an Inter-American System which includes the American declaration of Human Rights (of 1948), the American International Charter of Social Guaranties (of 1948), the Bogota Charter (of 1948). The Inter-American Commission on Human Rights and the Protocol of Buenos

Aires were later added, to complete a system similar in form to those of Western Europe.

The Socialist bloc was not left behind in the recognition of the importance of the international protection of human rights. The majority of the socialist countries have ratified the two covenants on Human Rights. And some of their constitutions have incorporated declarations involving human rights i.e. 1977 Soviet constitution.

In Africa, there is the African Charter on Human and People's Rights. This point brings to mind the issue of "third-generation rights" such as the rights to developments, rights to a general satisfactory environment, etc. Within this region of the world, human rights have been used as an instrument of change, an instrument against colonialism and oppression, an instrument of liberation and emancipation. Contrary to human rights being perceived as an instrument to preserve the status quo, it was seen (and used) and now being used as an instrument of change and aspiration for a more just and humane society. Future discussion of human rights will continue within and among classes within human society - thereby creating some dialectical relationship and probably producing generations upon generations of rights.

Africa after independence have witnessed a tremendous disillusionment and socio-economic and political failure resulting from corruption and the abuse of power which have led to atrocities, including gross violation of human rights. It is an irony that several new states in Africa at independence included in their constitutions, chapters on fundamental freedoms[4].

The irony is that, many advocates of human rights on the continent, who foresaw potential and the possible trend in the use of power by the African leadership and the potential effect it may have on human rights, advanced that adequate protection of human rights was the only solid basis for any new society[5].

However, the charter of the Organization of African Unity (OAU) later proclaimed that "it is the inalienable right of all people to control their own destiny" and affirms that "freedom, equality, justice and dignity are essential objectives for the achievement of the legitimate aspirations of the African peoples[6]".

The 1960's saw the proliferation of regional seminars and conferences with main themes focusing on the creation of bodies to deal especially with any form of human rights violations and arbitrary acts of governments[7]. By the early 70's, moves were already underway to establish a regional human rights institution. And the OAU reached an agreement for a charter to deal with the problem of human rights in Africa, with emphasis on the "people's rights," the duties of individuals, the institutions that will promote and protect human rights, the creation of obligations on state security and the methods of application of the provisions within the proposed charter.

The charter of 1981 contained 68 Articles and proceeds from a global and community approach to human rights, by translating these factors by way of rights and duties[8]. In traditional Africa, rights are inescapable from the idea of duty. The African form of humanism found expression in the "religious respect for others and the recognition of the rights and freedoms of everyone and of the entire group."

African liberties admits of necessity, the concept of soliditary which in turn generates duties towards others, to the community at large where he lives and to his entire surroundings. Therefore to an African, there are no individual rights without any corresponding duties[9].

On whether economic rights should take priority over civil and political rights - an idea which many African leaders have supported in many international gatherings[10], one should take cognizance of the fact that both sets of rights are not sequential but interactive.

It is one of the basic tenets for human rights in Africa that, basic economic needs must be secured before political liberties can be allowed. But, economic subsistence ought to be a basic right in itself[11]. Many leaders have however argued in favour of such a propos priority of economic development, stating that the state is fragile and many of the policies which has failed, has been those committed to providing political participation and freedoms.

But many leaders use this premise to eliminate opposition and therefore have the unlimited access to the plundering of the various economies. Corruption is rampant, thereby reducing the economic growth and keeping the right of the peasants in perpetual limbo although there is no clear connection between political authoritarianism and economic development.

Hawlett, basing her arguments mostly on Latin America, saw a positive connection between political repression and economic growth, but a negative connection between repression and "development" including redistribution[12]. But an authoritarian model of development is yet unproven[13].

Without human rights, there may not be economic developments but probably economic growth[14] and the question boils down to whether an

African concept of human rights really exists and if it does, it is expected to be home grown and indigenous.

The African Charter of Human and People's Rights, emphasizes the ideal of people's rights, at the possible expense of individual human rights - this is a great danger because it could be used by the power elites to manipulate and therefore oppressed the masses[15]. But in African societies, there exist a communitarian ideal within which the group is more important than the individual.

Decisions are made by consensus rather than by competition and economic surpluses are generated and disposed of on a redistributive rather than a profit-oriented basis. This description is more likely to fit in more with pre-colonial Africa and to assume an ideal such as that of human rights can be based on such a premise in 20th Century Africa, is an illusion and a different issue. It could be argued however, that, the so-called "African concept of human rights" is actually a concept of human dignity.

What we witness in Africa today, is nothing to write home about. No desire for economic development of a country can ever justify such a gross violations of human rights[16]. The realization of the new international economic order is very important and essential to economic development but the lack of it should never justify acts of torture, arbitrary arrests, killings and assassinations of political opponents and innocent citizens in many parts of Africa (and also in some part of the world).

Economic, strategic and national interests should not be used as a pretext by some powers and states, for perpetuating violation of human rights either within or outside their territories or within their areas of influence. Developing countries in order to make necessary progress towards both economic development and adequate protection of human rights within their territories need to democratize their political system so that their citizens can be productive and free.

Violations of human rights does not come only from the nations themselves but also from other sources as well . The phenomenon of terrorism, although often the direct consequence of state and/or governmental actions, is exercised on other occasions by individuals acting not only under the orders of a state (or government),but some other non governmental organization which shows the seriousness of the dangers to which human rights are subjected in the present World Order. We have seen violations involving multinational organizations such as Shell, like in the case of the

Ogonis, in south-eastern Nigeria, which led to the hanging of human right activist Ken Sarowiwa and others.

The violent impacts of terrorist acts and certain governmental action raises the issue of, the "inalienable status of rights."(inalienability of rights) According to Blackstone, this "does not entail the inalienable status of the exercise of that right i.e. the human right to equality of consideration and care," he argues that it is inalienable, but the exercise or instantiation of these rights in terms of income, education, medical treatment and so on can be alienated or denied for a variety of reasons.[17]

The purpose of the classical doctrine of universal inalienable human or natural rights was to rule out the conceptual possibility of ever treating a person as if he had no intrinsic worth. Therefore, the most important achievement of the universal declaration, is arriving at a concept consecrating a common standard of mankind for human rights beyond theoretical and practical differences on the nature of man's rights and freedoms.

The recognition of existing realities should not cause us to deny or disregard the step forward but rather to appreciate the importance of the progress achieved during the last forty-eight years in universalizing, the promotion, the guarantying and the respect for human rights. The problems that the implementation of human rights faces are many but it all stem from the fact that the violations of law is inherent to human society and freedom constitutes a goal which can never be entirely secured. This is the hard reality of the world we live in- a technoworld of the state of nature. It is the reality and trying to understand it that constitute the second part of this exercise.

Vincent said "human rights are the rights that everyone has, and everyone equally by virtue of their very humanity[18]",and this inherent attribute should be the framework of all instruments - international or national, aimed at protecting and enhancing human rights in our world today.

Chapter 6

HUMAN RIGHTS IN THE DEVELOPING AREAS OF THE WORLD: THE CASE OF AFRICA

Though the respect for promotion and protection of human rights presuppose the importance of human dignity possessed by every individual but one must not ignore the concept of human right and its relationship with the political society (and socio-economic factors and other forms of legal protection), and its potential to evolve and change with the course of time[1]

What then is the significance, and above all the efficacy of these international conventions for the protection of human rights?[4]. Especially when one considers the issue of whether the conditions (and patience) of some societies are better able to ensure application of the terms of the universal declaration of human rights or not. Or whether some others still need to go through an adaptive phase. The significance of this lies in the fact that when we refer to a human being - it is universal and nothing differentiates, one who by nature of the moment in life, finds himself in society A and the other in Society B.

Since the rights considered as human, is inherent in each individual, they - all human beings, should be so respected and protected wherever they may be on earth. It is only within this context and this spirit can we effectively do justice to this important principle. Human Rights have been given such prominence since the end of the Second world war and violations of human rights is considered a threat to international peace. But actions taken to redress these violations are not enough (if there are any at all). Reactions and responses to violations should not be selective and neither should it be limited to some powerless states.

Some powerful and influential states use their economic and intelligence agencies to carry out atrocities in less fortunate societies without regard to the well-being of the people in them. Such was the case in Rwanda, Afghanistan, South Africa, Namibia and Panama, to mention just a few.

The response of the international community should combine information and mobilization of opinion (involving non-governmental organizations, such as Amnesty International and Inter-rights and the international media in a non discriminatory fashion) in an effort toward universal enforcement. International conventions should also be developed to cover subjects of armed groups which have recourse to violence so as to distinguish "gangsterism and destructive nihilism from authentic opposition to arbitrary behaviours by those in power[3]."

But the universalism of human rights will always questioned. And this manifest itself in provisions such as those regarding the particular age set for voting or marriage without parental consent or the particular rules of inheritance which hardly seems to have human right status. While on the other hand, the United Nations' universal declaration include particular provisions such as periodic holidays with pay (Article 24), and security in event of disability or widowhood (Article 25). It also to supports claims that human rights are primarily rights of human beings.

Fundamental human rights should be inalienable, regardless of the arguments for legal recognition and regardless of whether there exists a "higher" natural law of which human beings are obliged by God to obey. These rights are part of the potential, that we have as living persons, even if they do not express that we are at any given moment in our lives. The recognition that these rights are part of each one of us emphasizes the "equality" of human beings whatever their national, racial or sexual differences[3.2].

The oneness between humans and its rights was also emphasized by Ed. Sparer when he wrote that, "we cannot give these rights away - we cannot "alienate" them - any more than we can give away a part of ourselves. We certainly can deny them to ourselves and to others. But when we do, we deny a part of ourselves and a part of others. We can act as if these rights do not exist, we can stop dissenting and thinking critically. We can stop developing our own free conscience and we can stop associating with our fellow humans in common struggle. But if we stop expressing these parts of our humanity, we become "alienated" human beings because we would be suppressing a piece of ourselves or complying with the effort of others to suppress us[3.3]".

Critical legal theorists do believe in values of human self-determination, speech, dissent and association, but there is a tendency to "disparage" the notion of "legal," "inalienable" and "universal" rights as a "means of addressing those values". But there those among them who critic the 'egoistic' nature of such rights as well as those who stresses the contradictions between the values of equality and self-determination.

The "egoistic," or "privalistic" content of individualistic and liberal rights, of speech and dissent are, according to Sparer, necessary for social struggle and advancement in both socialist and capitalist societies[4]. There is no inconsistency in the idea that some parts of the globe developed social and cultural patterns which support human rights (for example, the individualistic orientation of human rights) earlier while other parts of the globe developed more intensively, the social-cultural patterns that supports familial or other group orientation whose rights (- such as the right of the family to arrange the children's marriage) which may not be acceptable as human rights(which is in fact an example of the predominance values of Judaeo-Christian and western traditions over human right regimes). Although Pollack considers, "such localism " as that of development as against the regionalization of human rights[5].

Human rights from all indication should be the general "axiom" from which all other rights would be derived while the bills of rights should be in response to particular situations in our societies. For example the American and the French bills of rights were directed against tyranny and the UN Declaration emerged from the whole context of World War II, when the world faced Nazi's racist brutality and genocide. The Conventions against colonialism and racial discrimination are also examples of this type of response. Rights enunciated within these Conventions and agreements have their force in the barriers they would break down and the discrimination they would remove and the opportunities they would create (and of course, in the process creating other focal points in a process that may continue for ages). It is within this context that we should perceive the "third generation" rights because, while many of the established legislative actions ignored rights to a sound environment or a right to development, the situation in the world today, makes it imperative for us to care for the environment in which we live and we could clearly understand the potential impact of our continued degradation of it on our future. At each historical point in the formulation of a list or a demand for a right, some rights or items that are incorporated or omitted are not questioned because they are central to the movement(or forces) that produced the list. But in a dialectical process, demand for newer human rights will emerge, in addition or in replacement of older ones, as they constitute a response to the development in time.

For example, one of the rights that may lose its human rights status in the global upsurge of population is that of having children at will - beyond a reasonable number. While there are disincentives in certain societies, some are legalizing abortion, as a means of recognizing this phenomenon.

Quo Tendimus? -, the modern theoretical proponents of the rights of man do not see a particular formulation definitive. The rationalist sees human reason in the forms of intelligence, physical condition of men and evolving new and modifying old propositions for human rights. There should be no reason why by the next millennium, there shouldn't be another new sets of "generations of rights," which will be reflecting the development of that time. Human rights should therefore be seen as a derivative of the society that we live in at a particular point in time.

This phenomenon(derivativity of rights) should not reduce the qualities or inherent characteristics of the human rights. In other words, it should help in the process of implementation and adequate standard setting at local level while recognizing the socio-cultural environment. The European convention is a good example of this and it has demonstrated the relative ease (than attempts at globalizing), at which progress could be achieved at associating regional efforts with international initiatives.

The African Charter is in the right direction too. But in its case, it brings into focus, the notion, that society confers upon its members whatever privileges or exemptions they enjoy. This might not find any comparable relevance in the so called western or civilized world. But this notion is as much universal, historical and geographical in human history[6].

The notion of deriving benefits from one's society is not new, but a dominant form of political concept in Christian Europe since the 4th Century. It is pattern which also prevailed in non-western countries too. Among different groups in Australia, Africa and South America, group or ethnic hierarchies and customs are understood to be sanctioned by the divine order or nature.

In these groups there are no recourse for individual rights outside group structure. Just like in the Marxist society where values reside in the social order, this notion makes it improper to talk of individual rights prior to participation in society, because one derives such rights as one contribute to the society (or community). This premise have been used to question why contemporary human rights theory is based on the fact that ultimate value resides in the individual, independent from and even prior to participation in any social or political collective.

Proponents of the notion, even go as far as citing, the earliest suggestion of this idea, which occurs in the Hebrew accounts which describe Adam, whose name means "humanity" as being created in the "image of God" written in the 7th Century BC (and probably told centuries earlier). This account implies the emotional equality of all human beings and supports the idea of rights, that all enjoy by virtue of their common humanity[7].

Henkin observed on the contrary that the concept of human rights does not occur in Ancient or Rabbinic Judaism and that "the Hebrew language did not have an authentic word for rights. The word for a right today (Z'Khut) originally connoted purity, virtue, innocence and was used for benefits received or even deserved, but did not carry the sense that one had these benefits, as rights... Judaism knows not rights but duties and at the bottom, all duties are to God[8]".

The law that developed among the people of Israel, based on the principle of equality and justice which could function to ensure what we would call human rights: such as the right of field workers to eat while harvesting (Deuteronomy 23: 25-25), limitations on slavery (Exodus 21: 2; Leviticus 25: 10,39); protection of female slaves from arbitrary assault or abuse (Exodus 21: 7-11) and universal education (Deuteronomy 6: 7, 11:19)[9].

In its provisions, the Koran enjoins equitable sharing of goods and property (17. 28-31), fair treatment of slaves and generosity toward the destitute (76.7-10, 23, 62)[10]. There are many Christian and Muslim traditions that could be used to support human right policy. Many elements from traditional culture of a people could be used to support or legitimize human right policies.

The principle of equality and human dignity can easily find consensus among people of various cultures i.e. within the Chinese religious and philosophical traditions, one can find in Taoist and Confucian sources ample support: - for the claims that in Confucius' words "within the seas all men are brothers" demonstrates the existence of the notion of equality.

In Buddhism the notion of equality could be drawn from the Buddhist declaration of "compassion for every living creature" and on traditional injunctions of justice while the Jews, the Christians and the Muslims can find in divine sources the support for the principles of justice and equality and of concern for human beings[11].

Given the nature and the importance of human immediate environments and in its interaction with others of his kind, it is essential for a human right policy to involve constructing its philosophical and religious basis, in terms that will speak to people of different cultures. And not belonging to people solely of different cultures, or of urban "civilized" environments because many of these values should appeal to all people everywhere, including the developing areas of the world.

Human Rights should not be raised only as an issue and as desirable the rights of people are already violated but it should be an issue demanding constant monitoring and immediate action on the part of the international community, national governments and non-governmental organizations as well as individuals. The new world order and the epidemic violations of human rights that we are witnessing around the world call for a corresponding action of the world community to establish an international court structured to take up the responsibilities that may arise from human rights abuse wherever they may exist on the globe.

The world is becoming more and more aware of the need to have an international court capable of responding to inter-state conflicts and violations of international law in a changing world. And cases such as that of Sadam Hussein's invasion of Kuwait and his violations of International treaties, the Bosnian situation, the atrocities in Somalia and Rwanda should precipitate immediate international response like a "Nuremberg" type trial.

But a precedence must have been set by the Bosnia war crime trial which is an indication of how permissive this new world environment is to establishing a lasting international conduct among nations. The interdependence of States in a post-cold war world, makes it imperatively necessary to increase the power of the United Nations in order to take responsible actions in a world that is likely to witness further inter-state and intra-state conflict (especially between or and within small states).

This new world also call for a reinforced regional approach to the resolutions of inter-state conflict.

The Organization of African Unity (OAU) for example, in an attempt to respond to the needs of people on the continent, adopted the African charter in 1981 (which came to force five years later). The OAU was responding to the growing importance of regional instrument and approach to guaranteeing human rights and as a result of witnessing the gross violation of human rights on the continent. Or as a means of gaining international respectability. Otherwise referred to as the Banjul Charter, it confers rights on people whose states are party to it or who reside within the jurisdiction of a state party to it (47 African states have ratified it and Cote' d'ivoire, Seychelles, Ethiopia, Mauritius and Namibia are yet to).

Created under the charter, is a Commission (African Commission) with a mandate to promote and protect human rights in Africa. The African Commission is the body entrusted with the powers and functions of implementing the rights, in the charter. These rights, could also be classified into first, second and third generations of rights.

Under the Banjul charter, the Commission (also located in Banjul, Gambia) has the mandate to promote human and people's rights, to ensure the protection of human rights under conditions laid down by the charter and to interpret all provisions of the charter at the request of the State party, an institution of the OAU or an African Organisation, recognised by the OAU. In response to these, the Commission has developed rules and procedures to facilitate its effectiveness.

The Commission which is made up of 11 members representing each of the subregion of the continent, can examine an allegation by any state party to the Charter who believe or have reasons to believe that another state has violated the provision of the Charter. But is highly improbable that any state will do such thing.

This mechanism is rarely effective in the protection of human rights, but individuals or groups of individuals and non-governmental organization (NGOs) has been the only possible source through which recalcitrant states could be brought before the Commission.

A draw back in the entire process is that the procedures are not only cumbersome but demand that all legal avenues should have been exhausted within the state in question before being brought before the Commission. Giving the socio-political and economic conditions within African States, the idea of exhausting all remedies, is impossible[12]. In many African states, the judiciary is controlled by the junta or group in power and the case of Ken Sarowiwa, recently hanged in Nigeria is a case in point.

The bases of universal inalienable human or natural rights was to rule out the conceptual possibility of ever treating a person as if he has no intrinsic worth. But African leaders have, since independence demonstrated their inability to provide the basic need for their peoples. Worse still, is the inability of the entire continental leadership[represented in the Organization of African Unity(OAU)] to protect the rights of African peoples. There has been continued massacre in Liberia, the ethnic cleansing in Rwanda, while there is an ongoing military dictatorships and authoritarian leadership in many African states.

Africa has been used here to demonstrate both the regional effort at protecting human rights and the futility of its implementation. This is very characteristic of many parts of the World, especially in those of areas where there is a lack democracy, where there is poverty, hunger and war as it is the case in many countries of Africa, Asia and Latin America.

The African situation underscore the ineffectiveness of regional solutions, thereby necessitating a complimentary global response, to pressure member states so as to enforce regimes and obtain a better human rights conditions on the continent.

PART II : HUMAN RIGHTS IN A NEW WORLD ENVIRONMENT

In part two, we shall be examining the problems of implementing human rights agreements in a new world environment. There will be an attempt to analyse the changes in the world environment and the growing concern for human rights violations and the inability to enforce implementation. This inability to enforce is illustrated through the examination of the questions of the domestic jurisdiction, sovereignty and the ineffectiveness and or difficulty of enforcing sanctions to induce the fulfillment of membership obligation within the international system. These issues are directly linked to the questions of human diversity and the attempt at universalizing human rights and how it affect application of agreements between member states.

Chapter 7

THE NEW WORLD ORDER

With the end of the cold war came uncertainties and challenges in world politics, albeit with a constant desire for human rights protection in a world plagued with a reckless abandon for it. While this century have been dominated by an interchanging dominance of war and peace, the implementation of human rights agreements remain the central piece of any requisite for preventing the former(war) and sustaining the latter (peace).

The quest for peace and security and the continue reoccurrence of socio-economic and political circumstances which underscore the constant abuse suffer by humans around the world reinforce the need to implement and defend rights already created. This quest is not lost to the major powers of the world despite the fact that until 1985, there has been an intense rivalry among them. The rivalry have produced scenarios of war and peace, which to many "rhythmically explain the rise and fall of great powers."[1]

Each global transformation brought about changes in the world. It reshaped the international system by creating and enforcing rules that preserved existing world order. It is however important to note that the dominant power within the global structure exclusively determine the priority to be place on implementing agreements within such an order. It is therefore a product of whether such promotion will sustain the hegemony of such power or bring about the demise of a declining power.

The end of the second world war did not mean an end to uncertainty and mistrust. On the contrary the uncertainty of the global environment gave birth to a far more greater tension between major powers. For example the difference between the United States and the Soviet Union and their allies paved the way for the cold war and with it came the advent of the nuclear weapon, which radically transformed the role that the threat of force and warfare would ever play in world politics.

Everything in global politics was then seen from the perspectives of the East versus the West and human rights discourse inevitably became a product of this environment. Despite the war time collaborations, these powers and their allies engaged in a "mutual disdain for the other political system and way of life"[2] and of course their conception of rights. Their ideology became the prism through which they see each other. They saw their own action only as virtue and in those of their adversaries they saw malice.

The hostility that characterized this period inhibit an effective grounding of human agreements and their implementation. Considering that it is only within the period, first as a result of the experience of the second world war, that human rights gained prominence in international discourse to the extent that it became an internationally acceptable regime among nation-states, it is also ironic that, the major obstacle to its realization is because of the condition within which it was nourished.

This period witnessed a relationship that can be characterized as mutually antagonistic because of the expressed desire to contain the influence of the other in many parts of the world. This situation led itself to the accommodation of gross violations of human rights, especially if it serve the interest of any of the powers. This situation was also undermined by the alliance formation between the powers which created the conditions necessary for possible escalation of international conflict. An example was the Cuban missile crisis.

This period was followed by a mutual recognition of the potential for total destruction as a result of the weapons of destruction amassed since the second world war. The resulting reapproachment brought about renewed dialogue and the demise of détente. Mikhail Gorbachev also came along in 1985 with a new "thinking" while embracing mutual global security. His reform (Glasnost and Perestroika {openness and restructuring}) introduced democracy and market economy in the Soviet Union while at the same time seeking cooperation and economic assistance from its foes. With these dramatic changes came the collapse of the Soviet Union and the devolution of its empire in eastern Europe.

The immediate post cold war era was characterized by a "liberty for excessive rivalry that had exacted enormous resources, strained economics and impaired power relative to other greater power"[3]This new world order also witnessed the uncertainty which also gave birth to tension between great powers(both declining and the remaining superpower). Instead of this being between the East and the West as the case was after the second world war, it was tension between all powers because; (a) of the unpredictability of the situations in many states in transition from their just acquired sovereignty as a result of the devolution of the Soviet empire and (b), the lack of predictability on the part of the only remaining superpower which in turn was handicapped by the lack of certainty in the world brought about by the lack of a common threat (i.e. communism) as was the case previously and the desire of the American electorate to focus all their energy on domestic agenda. The post cold war era may not immediately have guaranteed a peaceful future, it however provided the avenue for testing the potential for global implementation of human rights agreements (however deficient it may be). There is a reshaped world with different values in which collective effort become relevant especially in preserving collective security. This resolution was tested in 1990 when the allies led by the United States, forced Sadam Hussein of Iraq to relinquish his occupation of Kuwait.

There is no certitude whether there will be a greater respect for human rights in this new world environment, but by all indication there is a potential for a better reaction to violations than we have ever had. The global condition practically remain the same because it is dependent on what government chooses to do with one another. There is no independent international legal system, capable of enforcing agreements and international law. The system is defective because it depend so much on the behavior and attitude of those it is suppose to regulate.

There is a lack of formal legal institutions like those existing at the domestic level. There is a lack of legislative, executive or judicial power. Rules are only made when states willingly observe them. The existence of sovereignty constitute an obstacle to the effectiveness of international legal institution. If human rights agreement, such as the covenants, were to be effective international law, its application within the current world order could only depend on its universality.

The concept of universality on the other hand is undermine by the pluralistic nature of cultures and a lack of common virtue among men. But unlike other values, rights acquired as humans are inherently universal in as much as one is a human being, cultural pluralism should therefore not be strong enough to inhibit its recognition and implementation as such.

The most important limitation is probably the level of commitment on the part of member states and their desire to actually pursue their respective national interest. One should not ignore the existing socio-political and whether these institutions permit the necessary condition conducive to the recognition and actual implementation of human rights within a particular state.

Apart from agreeing on the agreement and the diversity of socio-political conditions among member states, perhaps the most singular problem that human rights implementation faces in this new world order, is the absence of a reliable procedure of identifying a violation and the lack of authority to enforce compliance .

The United Nations which is the only possible source of enforcement is handicapped by its charter, by its structural composition and by the dominance of major powers like the United States (the veto and power of the United States was demonstrated in the recent failure of the former Secretary - General Boutros

Boutros Ghali in his reelection bid and the election of Secretary-General Kofi Annan), thereby reducing its ability to adapt to changes within the new world order without unnerving some of the major powers.

THE UNITED NATIONS AND ITS HUMANITARIAN EFFORTS

The United Nations was and is still a victim of the rivalry between the powers since the second world war. Right from the beginning, the power of the major powers was guaranteed among others by the provision of the charter which limited the capacity of the General Assembly to mount collective action. The charter authorized the Assembly to initiate studies of the conflict situation and bring it to the notice of the security council with recommendation for peacekeeping initiatives.

The Charter also restricted the role of the Secretary-General to that of an administrative officer. Article 99, for example, confined him to simply alerting the security council to peace keeping situation and to providing support for peace keeping operations. These restraints among others, makes it impossible for the United Nations to launch its own initiatives without involving the powers who on the other hand teleguide the process, to their own benefit.

The new world environment have however given the United Nations a new lease of life, which if effectively utilized might metamorphosed into an expanded, more constructive and definite but independent role for the world body. In 1988, for instance, the Security Council resolution 598 provided the framework for settling the Iran-Iraq war but at the same time brokered the withdrawal of Soviet forces from Afghanistan while monitoring activities in Nicaragua and the independence of Namibia.

The security council resolution 678 also authorized "member states cooperating with the government of Kuwait, to use all necessary means" to coerce Iraq's withdrawal from Kuwait. But oil has got a lot to do with the involvement and the easy way the collective action in Kuwait was initiated and effectively carried out- uniform commitment due to overwhelming interest in Kuwait- the free flow of oil.

The question therefore remain whether the United Nations and the major powers will be willing to take such collective action, whenever there is a violation of human rights. There was no such action in Rwanda, neither was there such action in Bosnia or many other places around the globe. The salvation of millions of the poor, dispossessed and ordinary citizenry probably lies in the hand of Non- governmental organizations. The roles of the NGOs have changed in the new world order. Not only have they increased in number but they have become a force to be reckoned with on many issues and especially on issues concerning human rights. They have investigated violations of human rights, they have documented and presented reports before bodies responsible for such issues within international organizations but these institutions have in many cases failed to act and the response of the international community remain as slow as ever.

The United Nations remains the most viable way of promoting human rights by creating norms (which is the belief about what is proper) against indiscriminate violations of fundamental human rights. Not only does the UN create and promote through its agencies, conferences and resolutions, among others, the need to promote and respect human rights, it indulged its members to refrain from its violation.

The United Nations perform these functions through fact finding and neutral investigations. It also encourages regional approaches by serving as a global theatre for the discourse and solutions of issues relevant to promoting the ideals of the Universal declaration of human rights. The activities of the

UN commission, committees and centers for human rights and the secretariat have been of tremendous importance in the promotion of these ideals.

But there are limits to the effectiveness of the UN as it promotes human rights around the globe. The nature of the international system is one which lend itself to the fact that governments generally maintained their rights to support and promotes the ideals set forth in the charter and that the UN might seek to promote solely within the context of their national interest.

Though some of the human rights goals of the organization may be viewed as necessary for the collective security of all and therefore calling for the total support of member states, it remain therefore simply as a goal but not as a general priority. In terms of rhetoric's both at national and international levels, human rights is a priority but in terms of policy implementation it remains everything but that. The ideals are set forth in declarations and convenants but these are constraint by certain limitations.

Chapter 8

CONSTRAINTS ON IMPLEMENTATION

The post cold war environment is characteristically dominated by major powers with the United States of America as the "top dog" and as Richard Stoll and Michael Ward described it, "a major power is a state that has interests, and the power to influence actors in pursuit of these interests, in other regions of the world as well as its own"[1]. The new world environment dominated by the United States and other major powers, remains one in which there is a slow response to human rights violations.

Since the end of the cold war, we have witnessed extensive human rights violations in Bosnia and Rwanda but with no matching response from the international community. Although neither the United States nor Russia felt it necessary to support regimes violating human rights in order to secure allies against each other, they have not gone out of their way to take dramatic action against violators either.

This should not surprise anybody and according to Jack Donnelly, human rights violations are in large measures an exercise of sovereignty which typically involve acts of states against their own nationals on their own territory,[2] progress in terms of respect for human rights rest fundamentally within national action.

This is true to the extent that such violations do not have a spill- over effect such as refugees fleeing prosecutions, thereby threatening international peace and security. Or if such acts are seen as contradicting internationally acceptable norm. The question raised by the sovereignty and domestic jurisdiction has been an obstacle in the implementation of international agreements, especially human rights, which should be a binding international standard without any self-selected national exemptions.

While there is an effective human rights promotion, there has been a far less effective forms of monitoring and enforcement. The absence of an effective monitoring and enforcement procedures undermine human rights regimes. And if regional regimes are dogged by the same problem they become ineffective as well.

The United Nations as the main organization with the responsibility of monitoring human rights, from its inception established the Commission on Human Rights to evaluate human rights world wide and investigate complaints.

The UN Commission and its Sub-Commission on Prevention of Discrimination and Protection of Minorities discuss violations and set up fact-finding groups. Through the Commission the United Nations have initiated several actions to promote human rights world wide. It has provided governments with experts, training programs and fellowships to promote observance of human rights.

There is also a UN High Commissioner for Human Rights with the mandate to promote and protect human rights world wide, work with governments to improve human rights, coordinate UN human rights activities and publicize human rights programs.[3]

The UN has the prerogative in humanitarian assistance as well as it does in promoting human rights, either in principle or in reality. The United Nations should double its efforts by responding more to the activities and monitoring carried out by the non-governmental organizations.

The UN is well equipped and possess the necessary institutional structures for promoting human rights across the globe but it should also strive more in the area of preventive diplomacy in order to prevent violation of human rights by its members. Important recognition should be accorded existing NGOs who continue to assist the organization because their annual reports and monitoring activities should be enough to initiate a preventive and effective diplomatic response to pursing violation of human rights agreements before they get out of hand and become cancerous.

Such immediate action would have prevented the calamity we saw in Burundi if the organization has heeded the Secretary-General's "overt preference in the Burundi situation for serious consideration to be given to the preventive deployment of troops to the area, or at least the issuance of a public warning by governments that they will intervene if a Rwanda-style massacre were to occur"[4]. The reluctance of the UN to undertake actions like this not only undermine its credibility but makes impossible to measure the impact of such an action.

Actions like this-"effective-preventive action" require a high degree of political commitment like we saw during the Gulf War but the United Nations has to be ready to compel governments contributing troops as well as back up in order to render the threat of force or the use of force effective. A preventive policy might even work in preventing an eventual peacekeeping because some of such threat would have been reduced by such effectiveness.

The Secretary-General's commitment as indicated in its agenda for peace reinforced the danger in the organization's involvement in national affairs. The UN involvement in this way is consider a potential political minefield but as the organization an important actor in a changed world, it become really important to step up actions against human rights violation as a prevention for future acts of violence as we saw in Rwanda and Yugoslavia.

The United Nations will continue to have its greatest successes in non-political and technical activities such as combating illiteracy and disease and most of its efforts to prevent aggression and maintaining peace through collective security, disarmament and peaceful settlement of dispute will meet with little success. But it is in the area of human rights that the organization can effectively begin to exert its growing influence in a changing world. The UN does have a record of intervention in cases concerning the violations of human rights. Though extremely few, it however represents the potential for the UN in the area of enforcing compliance among its members.

Cases like those of the Ache Indians in Paraguay and the action taking by the Inter-American Commission on Human Rights (an organ of the Organization of American States), to demand the government of Paraguay to intervene in the reported violation committed against the Indians and to protect their rights, however weak it might have been, resulted in the Paraguayan government bringing to an end the massacre and underscore the importance of such international pressure.

In 1982, following the killings of hundreds of Palestinians in the camps of Subra and Shatila, the UN General Assembly adopted a resolution condemning the killings. But nothing came out of the condemnation and when the same situation repeated itself in 1986, nothing was done by the international community or the United Nations. Not enough indignation was shown in this case as the UN General Assembly did nothing in the Paraguayan massacre.

These two cases demonstrate a lack of resolve on the part of the UN and the international community to take the necessary step to condemn inhuman treatment. The lack of resolve resulting from the weakness of the UN General Assembly and the politics of the veto within the organization [5]. The degree of incompetence shown here couldn't have been better reinforced than in the speech given on the 29th of September 1979 by the President of Uganda at the UN General Assembly when he said:

> Our people naturally looked to the United Nations for solidarity and support in their struggle against fascist dictatorship. For eight years they cried out in the wilderness for help; unfortunately, their cries seemed to have fallen on deaf ears. The United Nations looked on with embarrassed silence as the Uganda tragedy unfolded. Meanwhile, the Amin Regime continued with impunity to commit acts of genocide against its own people.."[6]

His words are very much true about the UN response to many situations around the world today.

The only response has been coming from the NGOs, who in many cases are doing it at the risk to their personnel. The increased activities of these non-governmental actors in international politics have been felt tremendously in the area of human rights and humanitarian intervention. They have been able to identify and locate situations where right have been violated. They monitored and make reports of such incidence available to international bodies. The questions of domestic jurisdiction and sovereignty have hindered the ability of international organizations such as the UN but not necessarily the NGOs. Human rights violation is either a result of governmental activities to retain control or dominate its citizens or a result of anti-governmental activities in a state of conflict within a society.

And in many cases, NGOs find themselves caught between helping the helpless at the risk of loosing the support of the authority by informing the outside world about violations of human rights and signaling to their humanitarian counterparts to begin preparing for possible disaster and crisis situation.

But if situation like those described above still continue, it is because governments (and member states) have been less than forthcoming in supporting implementation of human rights agreements.

It is the government or their agents (or as a result of actions of either or both) who authorizes, tolerate and practice torture and violations of human rights. And practices such as these continue because of the lack of the application of an international standard or norm. Trust must be established and enforced by member states through the exercise of constant, uniform and unbiased pressure over governments that violates human rights.

The case of apartheid in has been used to demonstrate the incompetence of the world community in its response to gross violation of human rights. The South African saga will remain an important measure of the United Nations impotence in the face of crime against humanity in its first fifty years.

The persistent inability of the world body to actively engage preventing violation of human rights after the lesson learned from South Africa raises the issue enforcing compliance with membership obligations within international organizations.

ENFORCING COMPLIANCE WITH MEMBERSHIP OBLIGATIONS

There is an extensive literature about sanctions as an effective mechanism for enforcing compliance with membership obligations within international organizations[7]. According to Woodrow Wilson in 1919:

If any member of the League of Nations breaks or ignores these promises with regard to arbitration and discussion, what happens, war ?. No, not war, but something more tremendous than war. Apply this economic, peaceful, silent, deadly remedy and there will be no need for force. The boycott is what is substituted for war.[7a]

Despite his optimism, a lot of controversies surround the effectiveness of these measures, its legal implication, its importance in international law and its use as a means of enforcing compliance among member states. Sanction is the specific reaction of the community constituted by the legal order against delit [i.e. delit, obligations and responsibility are corollaries of the concept of sanction)and it is within this context that we shall examine its use for enforcing compliance to international standards.

Sanction, despite its different interpretation, is used quite frequently with the measures of enforcement undertaken by international organisations to relate their membership compliance with the provisions of such Organisation. It will be propitious to present a synoptic map for defining this concept within the realm of our discussion.

To some, it means one of or all of the following:[8]

1) structural element of a standard of international law pinpointing the unfavourable consequences in the event of its violations.
2) Enforced measures taken by international organisations primarily the UN.
3) special political form of the state's responsibility in consequence of an international crime.
4) Individual and collectively enforced measures taken in retaliation to a delit.

Measures of compulsion used against a state that shuns its responsibility for its breach of law.

However, sanction will be considered to be (i) all or some of the above and (ii) a "negative measure which seeks to influence conduct by threatening and if necessary imposing penalties for non-conformity with the law."[9] . A sanction is therefore a legal term which indicate steps to be taken when a legal obligation is breached.

According to Kelsen[9a], sanctions are the specific reactions of the community, constituted by the legal order, against delits. And delit, obligation and responsibility are corollaries of the concept of sanction. A certain behaviour becomes a delit, if it is a condition of a sanction. Appropriately, a certain behaviour is the content of a legal obligation, if the contrary is a condition of a sanction and therefore a delit.

In the establishment of an obligation, certain behaviours are characterised as desirable and others undesirable, by formulating a prescription or a prohibition and this entirely constitutes a sanction. Another element in this whole process is obligation - it must be noted that an obligation is imposed upon the subject separately from the sanction provided. In order to establish a legal obligation a sanction must be attached to the contrary behaviour. These two concepts are therefore interdependent.

For example, it will be appropriate to know what obligations are provided for (or prescribed) by the United Nations. In Article 2 paragraph 2 of the

United Nations Charter, is the provision of an obligation of members to fulfil all obligations as stated in the said Charter.

According to the provision:

"All members, in order to ensure to all of them the rights and benefits resulting from membership, shall fulfil in good faith, the obligation assumed by them in accordance with the present Charter"[10]

The phrase of this article and paragraph 2 "in order to ensure to all of them the rights and benefits resulting from membership" imply that obligations must be fulfilled in order that the corresponding rights may be ensured. It demonstrate the dynamics of the sanction- obligation relationship [or vice-versa] because to impose an obligation on members also demand an enforcement action to be taken by the Organisation in case of contrary conduct . Sanction is therefore the end product.

Another obligation imposed on members by the UN Charter is that concerning the obligation to carry out the decisions of the Security Council.[11] Article 25 state that:

"The members of the United Nations agree to accept and carry out the decisions of the Security Council in accordance with the present Charter".

This imply that members are "obliged" to carry out the decisions of the Security Council, thereby demonstrating the contractual character of the obligation established by this provision [just like all other obligations established by the charter].

An overall examination of the charter reinforced the effect that the obligation entered into by the contracting parties are binding and a breach of which is likely to command an enforcement measure or a sanction. It could be deduced from Article 4 which is a follow up of Article 3 on the original membership of the UN, that membership in the UN is open to all other peace loving states which accept the obligations contained in the present charter and in the judgement of the Organisation are able and willing to carry out these obligations.

The above article placed prime importance on the compliance of the members - a condition to which they must accept before joining the

Organisation. Another important Article which is relevant to our analysis is that of 94, paragraph 1, concerning the obligations of members and other parties to the statutes with respect to the court. It stipulates that:

"Each member of the United Nations undertakes to comply with the decision of the International Court of Justice in any case to which it is a party"[12]. See Article 94 (2) also.

Although this is considered to be conditional because the members of the UN are not obliged to submit their disputes to the court. But they are obliged to comply with the decisions, not only with "the decision" of the court, if they have submitted their dispute to the court. This is not only an obligation of the members of the UN but of all parties to the statutes which are not members of the UN and even the states to which the court is open to under Article 35, paragraph 2 of the statutes.

It is also important to note that there are different forms of sanction and that they are gradual depending on the degree of the seriousness of crimes committed or the seriousness of the violations involved. In compliance with the provisions and enforcement procedures within the different international organisations, a sanction can be in form of the following:

1) Embargos [Economic, diplomatic, military etc.] -as stated in Article 41 of the UN Charter is a measure not involving the use of force and not involving expulsion or suspension.
2) Exclusion - which is considered as a limited sanction.
3) Suspension.
4) Expulsion or withdrawal ["compulsory" or "forced"].
5) Military force - the most grievous and in the last resort that can be applied under the UN Charter.

EMBARGO

This is an order issued by state authorities in one country that limits, interrupts or terminates its economic relations with another country. Embargo on the import and or export of all or particular goods, weapons and currency, on the transfer of scientific and technical information, copyright and other rights and some types of commercial and other economic activities may be applied in contemporary international relations as a means of economic or financial pressure, compulsion or reprisal[13].

Embargo is commonly used by international organisations to enforce compliance among its members. The UN Charter provides for the use of collective embargo as a reprisal with respect to a state whose actions constitute a threat to international security. It may be introduced both in times of peace and war, and may serve as a ground for suspending or ceasing all or some concrete commitments made by organisations or individual nations to the country concerned.

The covenant of the League of Nations, for example, provided for economic and military actions under Article 16, paragraphs 1 and 2 and the UN Charter in Article 41 call for measures that can be taken to correct a situation considered threatening to international peace and security by the Security Council which may include:

"..complete or partial interruption of economic relation and of rail, sea, air, postal, telegraphic, radio and other means of communications and the severance of diplomatic relations..." or and other actions that the Security Council might authorize state members to apply. This could involve embargoes such as oil, military or arms, ammunition, etc. This form of sanction, classified as "mandatory" and " comprehensive" was recommended against South Africa.

EXCLUSION

This is sometimes referred to as a limited sanction because it involves exclusion from some organs of an agency while the state is allowed to retain its representation on others[14]. Article 19 of the Charter of the United Nations for example deprives a state two years in arrears in its financial contributions to the UN or its vote in the General Assembly, but it allows it to retain a vote in the Security Council and to continue its representation in the Assembly. However, there is no provision in the Charter for excluding a member from the Councils of the Organisation or from any subsidiary organs. But it must be noted that the right to vote in The General Assembly is only one of the rights of membership but a very important one too which include the right to participate in election since the act of election include the act of voting[15].

SUSPENSION

Under Article 5 of the United Nations charter, a member may be suspended from the exercise of the rights of membership. According to this article:

"A member of the United Nations against which preventive or enforcement upon the recommendation of the Security Council. The exercise of these rights and privileges may be restored by the Security Council."

The suspension from the exercise of membership rights, does not mean an exercise of the rights which a nonmember state has under the charter [not comprising the statute]. The suspension from the exercise of the membership rights therefore, may at least temporarily place the member concerned in a position worse than that of a non-member.

EXPULSION [OR WITHDRAWAL - "FORCED" OR "COMPULSORY"]

Expulsion is another form of sanction which could be a withdrawal, in this sense forced or compulsory, as the case may be depending on the situation necessitating such an action. An expulsion from an Organisation is an enforcement measure in so far as it is an action taken against the will of the state concerned.

It must also be noted that, it is not the same thing as voluntary withdrawal. Expulsion is a sanction, for it is expressly directed against violation of an agreement (i.e. the charter) or more exactly against a member which has persistently violated the principle contained in the charter (or agreement).Another form of sanction involve the use of military force.

MILITARY FORCE

Considered as the other extreme end of the sanction continuum, the use of armed forces is to be taken as a last resort to enforce compliance of membership obligations. The Charter of the United Nations requires members of the Organisation not only not to resort to war against each other but to refrain from the threat or the use of force and to settle their disputes by peaceful means (Article 2 par. 3 and 4).

The effectiveness and the compliance with this obligation by members, since the inception of the Organisation is a totally different issue. But the use of force as an enforcement action is allowed by the charter in principle only as a reaction of the Organisation against a threat to the peace or a breach of the peace (Articles 39, 41 and 42). And as actions of the members, it is permitted only exceptionally in the exercise of self-defence (Article 51).

According to Kelsen, "If the enforcement action provided for by Articles 39, 41, 42 of the Charter are true sanctions, the Charter is at least in principle in conformity with the bellum justum doctrine"[16] - which implies just war. In other words, the only peaceful way of sanctioning non compliance with membership obligation involves other forms with the exception of the use of military force.

The question then remains as to what extent international organizations have responded, through its provisions and in practice to the issue of enforcing compliance among its members.

LEAGUE OF NATIONS

The covenant of the league of nations contained an express provision for the expulsion of any member. Article 16 paragraph 4, stated that any member of the league "which has violated any covenant of the League may be declared to be no longer a member of the league by a vote of the Council concurred in by the representatives of all the other members of the league represented there on"[17]. Many reasons have been given for the inclusion of this provision and among them is the need to prevent a state which after breaking its covenant still claims to vote on the council or in the Assembly of the League hence blocking any action of the League requiring a unanimous vote of the Council or Assembly.

Another reason is the need to terminate the membership of a member failing in its duty to pay its contribution.[18] A very good example of a country expelled from the League is the Union of Soviet Socialist Republics. It was as a result of its attack on Finland on November 30 1939, on the pretext of assisting the new government of the "Democratic Republic of Finland" to liquidate "the very dangerous seat of war created in Finland by its former rulers."

After a formal protest from the Finnish government and the matter transferred to the Assembly, the latter proposed a formal protest against the Soviet Union for the violation of the principle of the League of Nations. Giving the weakness of the league regarding the imposition of economic and military sanction, it opted to exclude the Soviet Union from the League[19]. Although there was a lack of unanimity required for such a decision, the Soviet Union was expelled because it has "placed itself outside the League of Nations"[20].

The expulsion of the Soviet Union automatically expelled it from all subsidiary bodies of the League but its failure to notify the International Labour Organisation about the continuation of its membership led to the cessation of its membership of that body too[21]. Another aspect of this case revolves around the fact that the provision on expulsion did not contemplate releasing a state from its duties under the covenant, but intended instead to subject it to an exceptional degree of international control.

According to Jenks, expulsion was not to be considered a confession of "the complete inability of the League to restrain illegal conduct" nor "as a process of outlawry ... snapping all legalities with the League" but rather "a precautionary clause intended to enable the league to protect itself against obstruction by a covenant-breaking state..."[22]. In this case, the aggressor was absent from the meetings of the Council and the Assembly and did not make any effort to block the decision of the League.

But the League has proved ineffective in other similar cases, for example, the invasion of Ethiopia by Italy and the West German attack on Poland on September 1 1939, which was officially brought to the attention of the league's membership[23]. It could be argued therefore that the purpose of the expulsion clause is to provide a disciplinary sanction or to exert pressure on the recalcitrant state to fulfil its obligations under the covenant "as a condition of readmission to the privileges of membership."[24].

Other sanctions provided for by the League also include economic and military sanctions as stipulated in Article 16 paragraphs 1 and 2 of the covenant and enforceable only in case of a resort to war by a member of the League in violation of the covenants under Article 12, 13 and 15.

To Louis B. Sohn, expulsion in the League system has a triple function: (i) It served as a preliminary measure enabling the League to avoid a veto in any action to be taken under Article 16 paragraph 1 and 2; (ii) It could be used in place of the sanctions under those paragraphs or as the ultimate weapon if those sanctions should prove ineffective and (iii) its application was permissible in cases of violations not covered at all by the other paragraphs of Article 16.

The following obligations, if breached could lead to expulsion:

a) The obligation to respect and preserve as against external aggression the territorial integrity and existing political independence of all members of the League.

b) The obligation to register with the Secretariat of the League every treaty or international engagement entered into by any member of the League.

c) The obligation not to enter into any engagements inconsistent with the Covenant and to procure release from inconsistent engagements entered into prior to becoming a member of the League[25]. And further, the obligation to execute an arbitrary award[26], in case of refusal by a national parliament to execute a member's obligations under the covenant[27], in case of violation of Articles 22 of the covenant which governed the mandate system[28]. The applicability of this provision had been raised in connection with the obligation to contribute to the expenses of the League, "to secure just treatment of the native inhabitants of territories" under the control of the League. In fact, the USSR was expelled in 1939 on the formal ground that it "refused to be present at the examination of its dispute with Finland before the Council and Assembly" in violation of Article 15 of the covenant[29].

On the basis for expulsion under the covenant, it is argued by some that only "intentional" violations of the covenant could be the basis for the expulsion. But article 63 paragraph 4 did not so limit the discretion of the Council, but authorised it to expel any member which violated the Covenant, intentionally or otherwise. And any proof that the violation was not a result of deliberate governmental policy would be considered as a mitigating circumstance and might result in admonition rather than expulsion[30].

The jurisdiction to decide on expulsion lay with the Council of the League. It has been noted that a member did not lose its membership ipso facto as a consequence of a violation of its obligations under the covenant, but that, a specific decision of the council was required in order to deprive a violator of its membership. The council was not bound to expel a member even if a violation had occurred, it might do so if it found that the gravity of the case warranted such a severe sanction and its decision therefore becomes discretionary rather than obligatory[31].

The Covenant conferred jurisdiction with respect to expulsion exclusively on the Council and the Council was neither obliged to refer the matter to the Assembly nor to follow the Assembly's recommendation on the subject[32].

It has also been argued that expulsion required two separate decisions. First, a finding that a member has committed a violation of the covenant and second, a decision to impose the sanction of expulsion. The covenant expressly mentioned the second decision and was silent with respect to the first, nonetheless, the power to render the decision on expulsion implied the power to decide the preliminary issue of violation and the voting procedure applied in both cases[33].

THE UNITED NATIONS

The Charter of the United Nations does not use the term "sanction" but contains provisions that clearly stipulate sanctions, the first of which is Article 6 and the second is Article 19. Article 6 states that:

"A member of the United Nations which has persistently violated the principles contained in the present Charter may be expelled from the Organisation by the General Assembly upon the recommendation of the Security Council."

During the debate prior to the adoption of the expulsion provision, during the United Nations conference in San Francisco, some of the proponents of the provision believed that, though suspension might be an adequate sanction for misbehaviour in the typical case, "it is desirable to have a stronger penalty"[34].

This penalty, because of its severity would "only apply to member states which were admittedly incorrigible and which violated the principles contained in the Charter in a grave or persistent manner"[35] and it was argued that it would be "better to remove completely" such a nation rather than "let it corrupt the Organisation " so that such removal would "not increase the danger of international disorder" because the expelled nation "would still be bound by various obligations devolving upon non-member state"[36].

These arguments was carried, despite counter arguments[37]: that such a provision was inconsistent with the principle of universality which was a presupposition of the Charter; that it would force a member state to end relations with an expelled state, a consequence which might be practicably disadvantageous for a member state; that expulsion made reconciliation less likely and made more likely the development of centres of opposition to the Organisation around which other discontented states would rally; and that this provision was an unrealistic sanction which was bound in practice to prove less effective than a provision limited to suspension.

The jurisdiction for expulsion under the UN Charter is conferred on the Security Council. It is by its decision that it "recommends" the expulsion of a member to the General Assembly. This decision requires, in conformity with Article 27, paragraph 3, an affirmative vote of 7 members including the concurring votes of the permanent members. The decision of the General Assembly requires in its own turn, and in conformity with Article 18, paragraph 2, a 2/3 majority of the members present and voting.

Both decisions are necessary to bring about the expulsion of a member. The General Assembly is not bound by a recommendation of the Security Council to expel a member but the General Assembly cannot expel a member without a previous recommendation of the Council to do so. Also, the Security Council and the General Assembly are not bound by the Charter to inflict the sanction stipulated in Article 6 upon a member. The Article said they "may" expel a member found guilty by them of having persistently violated the principles contained in the Charter. But they may, for some reason or another, refuse to exercise this function.

The UN Charter also provide for the suspension of a member for violations of its obligation to the Charter, under Article 5. But the suspension of the exercise of the rights of membership could be an appropriate sanction against any violation of the obligation of a member. The Charter also allows, not only to deprive a member of most of its rights of membership, as a sanction, for persistent violation of the principles but to suspend a member, against which preventive or enforcement action has been taken, from the exercise of all its rights.

The charter provide for the suspension of a member from the exercise of a special right, in case of non-fulfilment of a special obligation, i.e. the obligation stipulated in Article 17 paragraph 2, to bear the expenses of the Organisation as apportioned by the General Assembly. The suspension of the right to vote is also provided for, under Article 19. There is a provision for enforcement measures (sanctions) by the Security Council, under Article 39, in case of noncompliance with any decision of the International Court of Justice.

Other provision include Article 102, paragraph 1 concerning sanctions for non-registration of Treaties with the Secretariat of the Organisation. In this case "no party to any such treaty may involve the treaty or agreement before any organ of the United Nations" - which implies a forfeiture of the rights which the unregistered treaty confers upon the party. Other enforcement measures provided for in Chapter VII includes the economic and diplomatic sanctions recommended in Article 41.

But any policy of sanction that is not universally applied and enforced stand a marginal chance of success[38]. Recently we have seen the United Nations successfully use military sanction against Iraq and the otherwise less successful "peaceful sanction" against South Africa. The enforcement of any sanction is dependent on the decision within the UN Security Council, the only organ which can enforce any sanction against any member state, in a situation of a "threat to peace", "breach of the peace" or an "act of aggression".

To effectively demonstrate the use of sanction as a result of violations of human rights, we shall use the attempts by the international community to enforce South African's compliance with international standard. The decision on sanction against South Africa was a direct result of its apartheid policy. The politics of apartheid in South Africa was a:

"system of racial discrimination built atop an immense foundation of economic exploitation, political repression and cultural obliteration, established and maintained by ruthlessly organized and executed violence of white against black."[39]

Apartheid was a policy based on white supremacy over the majority black. It was composed among others, such discriminatory act as, the Mines and Work Act- which reserved certain categories of work for whites only; the Native Urban Act- which restricted Africans to segregated residential areas and they could only move within these areas and those were white South

African lives, with the use of a "pass" (before it was scrapped and replaced by another effective means of controlling the movements of blacks).

The apartheid policy also include the Industrial Conciliation Act of 1924, which restricted the use of collective bargaining to whites and coloured people only. Central to this policy is that in South Africa and in the illegally occupied territory of Namibia, the blacks have no political or economic rights. And another source of conflict is South Africans occupation of Namibia.

For decades, the UN "patiently and persistently sought to persuade Pretoria to bring South-West Africa [Namibia] into the Trusteeship system and to fulfil its mandate obligation toward the people of the territory"[40]. Resolutions were adopted, special committees formed, negotiations carried out and the International Court of Justice (ICJ) devoted more time to the problem than any other. But South Africa was to move even further away from its commitment to a "Sacred Trust", seeking to dismember and annex the land and increasingly repressing its African majority.

The atrocious policies of the government of South Africa was a major concern for the United Nations since the inception of organization. The South African problem fell within the principles set forth in Articles 55 and 56 and the government of South Africa was condemned for breaching these principles. Moreover, the purpose of sanctions against South Africa was to induce necessary change within its domestic policy, in compliance with the ideals of the UN[41]. The provisions under Chapter VII of the Charter made collective sanctions the first alternative against the breach of legal obligations of the UN[42].

Article 42 provide a last resort, in which the use of force is implied. However, the first resolution made by the General Assembly recommending sanction was in response to the "Sharpeville massacre" in which peaceful demonstrators were killed in 1960. The Assembly recommended a comprehensive set of measures against the Pretoria regime, among these are:

-Severance of diplomatic relations with the racist regime

-The closing of ports to South African vessels

-A total embargo on trade[43].

In response to another incident, this time the 1976 "Soweto Massacre", the United Nations Security Council recommended that states should cease "forthwith, the sales and shipment of arms, ammunition of all types and military vehicles to South Africa".

During the period of ten or twelve years that followed the "Sharpeville" incident, many resolutions were passed and the International Court of Justice declared the presence of South Africa in Namibia illegal. But the United Nations Security Council did not take action under Chapter VII of the Charter until 1970, when it resolved that,

"....the military build up and persistent acts of aggression by   South Africa against neighbouring states seriously disturbs the   security of those states... and ... gravely concerned that South   Africa is at the threshold of producing nuclear weapon ... and   ... strongly the South African Government for its ... defiant continuance of the system of apartheid"[44].

This particular decision is of no consequence because the United States, UK and France abstained, rendering the UN decision ineffective because, when it acts under Chapter VII of the Charter, with the concurring votes of the permanent members, the members are obligated to carry out both the UN General Assembly resolutions and the UN Security Council recommendations. The fact must be emphasized that members are not committed to the principle of the Charter when it is contrary to their economic benefits. The economic interest of the developed countries in South Africa therefore played an important role in the implementation of the decisions of the UN and their support for it.

According to Colin Legum, western powers were in a fix about what to do with respect to South Africa:

"...of all trading and investor countries faced with a conflict   between economic and political interest where does the balance   lie? South Africa is not just a major Western trading partner   it is also the West's major source of strategically important resources."[45].

The combining role of the transnational corporation with their mother countries has helped to soften the impact of the sanctions of the United Nations. The problem of effective sanction against South Africa is because of the absence of a central executive organ in the international system. According to F.S. Northedge;

"The International system with its lack of central executive organs, is so structured that, if a state does not look after its own interest, it can be fairly sure that no one else will."[46].

There is an apparent desire on the part of member states for the ideals of the United Nations and to share its purpose of maintaining international peace and security but these desires are undermined by their preoccupation with their national interest which comes first before everything.

But these sanctions were not totally ineffective because through a series of efforts, the United Nations was been able to increase the world awareness of the existence of the South African policy. It was able to isolate Pretoria within the UN and the international system and by also pressuring South African's friends within the United Nations who in turn pressured her. These actions forced some changes in the position of South Africa although this was less than what was actually desired. But the sanctions, the pressures and the intensified action of the African National Congress (ANC) drove foreign investment out of Pretoria.

On the Namibia, the cost of the conflict with the South West African People's Organization (SWAPO), the end of the cold war and the intensified action on the part of SWAPO and the United Nations changed South African policy, leading to a transitional program and the independence of Africa's last colony in 1990.

The limitations posed by the factors raised above are as important as that of Article 2 (7) of the Charter, under which South Africa claimed domestic jurisdiction. The Article states that:

"Nothing contained in the present Charter shall authorise the United Nations to intervene in matters which are essentially within the domestic jurisdiction of any state or shall require the member to submit such matters to settlement under the present Charter..."

However, the article ended with a notation that:

"...this principle shall not prejudice the application of enforcement measures under Chapter VII."

Precedents and the rulings of the ICJ did not support the South African claim, that the UN is acted ultra-vires, when it ruled that "...when the Organisation, taken action which warrants the assertion that it was appropriate for the fulfilment of one of the stated purposes of the United Nations, the promotion is that such action is not ultra-vires the organisation."[47].

In some of its actions against South Africa, the United Nations through its Commission and Centre on Transnational Corporations was able to influence the activities of the multi-million giants (TNCs), who constituted the bedrock of South African economy. They (TNCs) reformed their policies and their activities, through disinvestment and some through the application of various codes of conduct.

It is however appropriate to conclude our discussion on constraints on implementation of human rights agreements by also examining attempts, by specialized agencies of the United Nations and other regional organizations, to enforce compliance among its members. The question of what happens when there is an expulsion of a state from a subsidiary or specialised organs of the United Nations while the state still retains its membership of the Organisation, is similar to the issue raised when the Franco Government of Spain was debarred from the membership of the UN because of its relationship with the AXIS power during the 2nd World War.

Spain participated in other conferences (especially the one bringing into force the International Civil Aviation Organisation) and keeping her out in the early days of the United Nations, necessitated its been debarred form the membership of the ICAO, to which it has been a contracting party [various steps were also taken by the United Nations to ensure that Spain did not become a member of other specialised agencies],which is a clear case of forced withdrawal[48]. The decision of the UN was revoked in 1950 and Spain became a member of the United Nations[49]. Other specialised agencies, especially the ICAO took necessary steps to re-establish relationship with Spain.

(A) INTERNATIONAL MONETARY FUND

The Articles of Agreement of the International Monetary Fund do not provide for expulsion in the actual sense but do provide for compulsory withdrawal, which can be described as expulsion in disguise. Section 2(a) of

Article 15 allows the fund to declare a member ineligible to use the fund's resources if the member "fails to fulfil any of its obligations under the Agreement"[50]. In addition, if after been declared ineligible the member persists in its failure to fulfil its obligations or a difference between a member and the fund concerning the par value of its currency continues, under Section 2(b), of Article 15, upon the expiration of a reasonable period, the "member may be required to withdraw from membership in the fund by a decision of the Board of Governors carried by a majority of the Governors representing a majority of the total voting power."

A good example of the application of these provisions was when Czechoslovakia recurrently failed to provide information concerning its national income and balance of payments which the fund was authorised to request. The situation degenerated in 1953 when due to this lack of information the fund's staff were unable to assess the implication of a change that Czechoslovakia had made in the par value of its currency. By December 31 1954, after which Czechoslovakia had not complied with the Executive Director's demand, on the ground that it was entitled to withhold information for reasons of national security, its recommended withdrawal was effected[51].

(B) INTERNATIONAL BANK FOR RECONSTRUCTION AND DEVELOPMENT

At the time of having problems with the IMF, Czechoslovakia was also having problems with the IBRD. The Articles of Agreement of the Bank made it, however, clear that once Czechoslovakia ceased to be a member of the Fund, it would "automatically cease after three months to be a member of the Bank, unless the Bank by three-fourths of the total voting power ... agreed to allow it to remain a member"[52]. But the Bank has commenced its own suspension proceedings in 1953 under a separate provision requiring automatic expulsion one year after suspension because Czechoslovakia never completed payment of its subscription to the Bank.

Having rejected a request for further postponement of this obligation, the Bank took action in September of 1953 when the Executive Directors recommended that Czechoslovakia be suspended. Its suspension was to take effect on December 31 1953, unless full payment was made by that time[53]. But it ceased to be a member a year later.

Other agencies may be categorised into three, depending upon their rules concerning expulsion(This is based on the work done by L.B. Sohn in, "Expulsion or forced withdrawal from an International Organisation", Harvard Law Review, Vol. 77, No 8, June 1964):

1) Those specialised agencies whose constitutions contain no provision on expulsion. Included in this group are; Food and Agriculture Organization [FAO], the parties to the General Agreement on Tariff and Trade (GATT], the International Atomic Energy Agency [IAEA], the International Labour Organisation [IL0], the International Telecommunications Union [ITU], the Universal Postal Union (UPU], the World Health Organisation [WHO], and the World Meteorological Organisation [WMO].

2) Those specialised agencies who link expulsion from the agency to expulsion from the United Nations i.e. The United Nations Educational Scientific and Cultural Organisation, provides in Article 2 that "members of the Organisation which are expelled from the United Nations Organisation cease to be members of this organisation."[54]. In fact, UNESCO's constitution contains no provision concerning expulsion of members of UNESCO which are not members of the UN. The International Maritime Organisation leaves the decision on expulsion of a member completely in the hands of the General Assembly of the United Nations. It's Article 11 provides that "no state or territory may become or remain a member of the Organisation contrary to a resolution of the General Assembly of the United Nations"[55].

3) The Third group belong to specialised agencies whose constitutions are patterned on the Articles of Agreement of the International Bank for Reconstruction and Development. A good example of this is the Articles of Agreement of the International Finance Corporation and of the International Development Association - their provisions states that a member suspended for a failure to fulfil any of its obligations "shall automatically cease to be a member one year from the date of its suspension", unless a majority of the Board of Governors decide to restore the member to good standing. Any member which is suspended from membership

or excluded from the Bank would automatically cease to be a member of both IFC and IDA.

SUBSIDIARY ORGANS OF THE UNITED NATIONS

-The Economic Commission for Africa - After considering article 19 on limited sanction under the Charter, there is no express provision in the Charter for excluding a state from the Councils of the Organisation or from any subsidiary organs. But the Economic and Social Council in 1962 was faced with the demands of African states that Portugal and South Africa be excluded from the Economic Commission for Africa - a subsidiary organ of the Council.[56] It was argued that both had refused to comply with various resolutions of the General Assembly and had committed grave violations of human rights in defiance of the principles of the Charter of the UN - violations which in some cases amounted to genocide.

And some members of the Commission found co-operation with those states on African economic and social problems impossible and expulsion was considered as the only remaining alternative. Taking the advantage of a South Africa's declaration, that it would no longer participate in the activities of the ECA, a resolution was approved which provided that South Africa "shall not take part in the work of the ECA until the Council, on the recommendation of the ECA shall find that conditions for constructive co-operation have been restored by a change in its racial policy"[57]. Portugal was expelled from the commission too.

REGIONAL ORGANIZATIONS:

The constitution of the Council of Europe, provided for the expulsion of members that seriously violated the obligation to "accept the principles of the rule of law and the enjoyment by all persons within its jurisdiction of human rights and fundamental freedoms..."[58]. The constitution of the league of Arab states under Article 18 paragraph 2 provide for expulsion of a member if it fails to fulfil the obligations imposed on it by the constitution. Article 26 of the Convention for European Economic Co-operation also authorises expulsion of a state for failure to fulfil the obligation imposed by the Convention.

The Charter of the Organisation of American states is one of the many constitutions which do not contain an express provision for expulsion. However, if the territorial integrity or political independence of any state is threatened, article 26 provide that certain procedures of the Rio Pact may be invoked and the organ of consultation called into session immediately to agree upon measures against aggression or for "the common defence and the maintenance of ... peace and security"[59].

In excluding Cuba, it was stated by the organs of consultation at Punta de Este on January 31 1962 and through its resolution VI, that the present Cuban government was incompatible with the principles and objectives of the inter-American system because of its identification with Marxist-Leninist ideology and its political, economic and military ties with communist nations; and it resolved that this incompatibility excluded that Government of Cuba from participation in the inter-American system. All the rejection and proposals were directed against the "present government of Cuba" and not the Cuban people - this is an ingenious solution which was considered as the adaptability of the inter-American system to unforeseen circumstances.[60]

The elasticity of the measures for enforcing compliance with membership obligations cannot be over emphasized and this has provided tremendous opportunity for its manipulation and its effectiveness in questionable But to Osieke, "in the growing body of international law of co-operation or welfare which is concerned with the development of methods of co-operations for common purpose, it is the privilege of membership and participation in the common activities which provide the essential sanction."[61]

The most effective sanction therefore, is that of non-participation. The exclusion from benefits conferred on the participants by the joint activities which is the effective sanction for compliance with the obligation undertaken. It is within the context of W. Friedman's theory of sanction of non-participation or "exclusion" that the evolution of contemporary international Organisation has added a new dimension to the general question of sanction in international law.[62] UN sanctions are symbolic, but the most manifest of these sanctions, are those made by financial institutions like IMF or the World Bank because it involves financial obligation, which states readily respond to. The only genuine sanction under the Charter is that considered in Article 6, concerning expulsion and Article 19 concerning suspension from the voting rights in the General Assembly.

Only four times in the history of the United Nations has the organizations use military force. Including its measures in the Security Council resolution 678(1990), when member states cooperating with the government of Kuwait were authorized to "use all necessary means" to uphold resolution 660 and all subsequent resolutions to restore international peace and security in the area.. It is evident however that sanction whether expressly provided for or implied helps to ensure effective enforcement of the laws of establishing institutions. And this could be an effective means of enforcing compliance with human rights agreements and violators of which should receive appropriate sanctions.

Chapter 9

THE QUESTION OF UNIVERSALITY

The problem with human rights is that it is complex in its conception as well as in its application. This characteristic has been one of the most important obstacle to the implementation of human rights regimes around the globe. The problem originate from the diversity in conceptualization as well as interpretation in a very diverse world. When critically examined, there should be no reason for the world not to agree on what constitute rights accruable by an human by virtue of the fact that he/she is human.

The question of the universality of human rights is central to the understanding, promotion and implementation of international regimes. From all indications, many human rights regimes start off from the simple premise that it serves humans. That rights as stipulated in the agreements, are recognized as belonging to all human beings at all times and in all places. Universality of these rights are implied for example, in the preamble of the universal declaration of human rights:

"... Now therefore the General Assembly proclaims this Universal Declaration of Human Rights as a common standard of achievement for all people and all nations to the end that every individual and every organ of society keeping this declaration constantly in mind, shall strive by teaching and education to secure respect for these rights and freedoms, and by progressive measures national and international, to secure their effective recognition and observance....."[1]

The mere suggestion that the declaration of these rights as a common standard of achievements for *all people* shows the desire that these should be the ideal standard " which every human community should try to reach"[2] It also shows that these rights which all people should have, is solely by virtue of their being human, irrespective of their nationality, religion, sex, social status, occupation, wealth, property or any other differentiating social characteristics.

The inherent universalism of human rights is reinforced as we explore the declaration further. In its article 2 there is also reference to entitled rights without any socio-cultural, political and economic "distinction". article 8 also affirms equality before the law because of its provision that "Everyone" not Europeans, not Americans or whites or Anglo-Saxons but "everyone" has the rights to an '.. effective remedy by the competent national tribunals for acts violating the fundamental rights granted by the constitution or by law'.

The use of the expression "everyone" in nearly all of the articles affirms its universalist intention. It is a reference to all people by virtue of their being human. It is erroneous to assume that only western and liberal democratic societies embodies these values because all human societies, wherever it may exist, exudes some of these values. The codification and the internationalization may have been a result of its diffusion from these western liberal-democratic societies but it not an ideal that exist solely within those societies.

The universal qualities of these rights accommodates adherence to common heritage as reflected in many regional regimes such as the European Convention and the African Charter on Human and Peoples rights because it allows peoples to strive to achieve the standard set forth in the declaration and the Covenants. The existence of these regional standard reflect the inherent universalism because it has become the ideal and the standard to strive for, however utopian it may seem.

The only tradition that these rights draws their constitutive values from is human being. There is first a human being before we have a society or a culture. The human being exist and others like him exist and develop ways of life and rules of interaction and customs and civilisation to support their existence. Human being is a product of socio-cultural milieu which exist because he created them. The socio-cultural milieu are a product of his understanding of himself. The socio -cultural milieu is mutable and it exist by virtue of his creation.

These rights are like other sets of rules which evolves as the human being understands himself and the values that he places on his /her own existence. The lack of ancient linguistic references to rights is not enough to base our assumption that those ancient civilizations have no moral qualms about such things. Just as well, we might assume that in ancient Rome, there were no others who felt the pains of the slaves.

At one point in the past, it was acceptable to enslave others but today, it is even unacceptable in some societies to deny women equal pay. Maybe our conception of rights accruable to human beings acquires some degree significance as we achieve some moral maturity as the human civilisation evolves.

We cannot ignore the diverse human conditions, such as our culture, language, etc., which are simply different ways of being human"[3], which is part of our cultural trait but does not mean that we are therefore a specie other than human. The idea that universal human rights may have started off as being an ideal or a minimum standard and the fact that its is applicable to all peoples irrespective of cultural or civilization differences, shows the moral justification in its universal application.

Using Kant's conception of universalisability- morality, the universalism of human rights as a moral standard makes it an obligation for human beings to respect it. Human beings do have intrinsic values which commands some moral justification for respecting his worth. The fact that rules are set to protect human life, confirms human conception of the sense of worth that is intrinsic in being an human being. Without human rights there will be no community because having a set of rights is part of belonging to a community. It is also the requirement of the community members to uphold and promote the interest of the community as part of their duty.

In doing so rights is intricately linked to being human which in essence dictate the nature of our society. The society that guarantees the rights of its members possess a higher moral values and has the potential to develop sense of responsibility and community.

In a new world order, the globe is shrinking because of the fall of physical boundaries through technological advances leading to dramatic changes across the world, making our unique cultural trait an object of interaction with many others. The universalism of the post cold war era is more embarrassing and less contradictory thereby creating the atmosphere for the promotion of human rights.

Whether the regimes in existence provide moral foundation for politics or concerned with the application of politics, it is however a process in the establishment of the principle of common morality in all human dealings with one another.

But when governments violates these moral codes by violating the rights of their citizens, shouldn't we be held responsible for doing nothing and are we not guilty because of our inability to sanction them. This is the question that the international community have faced for centuries because, time after time human societies only reacted after atrocities have been committed and afterward failing to prevent their reoccurrence.

The preoccupation of the human community in this new world environment should be finding the mechanism for effective implementation of these regimes. There are instruments in place for doing this, as we discussed in the last chapter but there are lots of possibilities as we move into the next century.

Chapter 10

THE FUTURE OF HUMAN RIGHTS AND ITS APPLICATION

Human rights should be seen as a protection to which all human being are entitled because of their humanity, not their social status or individual merit. These rights should be claimed and enjoyed without regard to any political order. In order to appreciate the problems facing the implementation of these rights, it is important to understand the fact that the same people that have the responsibility of protecting these individual rights are the same as those responsible for implementing them.[1]

The government is the enemy of human rights but preserving these rights is dependent on its (government) desire and ability to do so. The existence of these rights is a challenge to the authority of these governments. For effective realization of these rights might in some situation be a function of the good will of these authorities. Given the apparent hostility to rights, the only available remedy apart from depending on governments' goodwill is constitutional limitation in order enhance the prospect for preservation of human rights.

For this reason, constitutional democracy has the most potential in preserving human rights. This is not only true at domestic level but very much so at international level. Human rights regimes came into being as a result of the express desire of leading democracies to introduce a measure for attaining relative dignity for all human. As a result of this singular desire, human rights should also be use as a determinant of a state participation in international organizations. There should no rational for states, that have been condemned and sanctioned for violating international norms, to remain as members of United Nations and any of its agencies and committees. Representatives of these governments should be denied participation in any global international deliberation.

Human rights violations are mostly results of governmental actions to retain control or dominate its citizens and allowing such a government to seat with other human rights respecting states makes a mockery of the entire system. These central governments are very important in prohibiting rights violations and a self limitative action on their part will go a long way to enhance implementation of human rights regimes.

There have been positive developments since the end of the second world war, in the area, of adopting many recommendations of the universal declaration, the covenants and other regimes, as part of constitutions. The implementation of these instruments offers humanity tremendous opportunity. It offers the individual a free society in which he/she is free "to pursue their potential in relationship with others"[2]

Another dimension to the potential offered by these instruments was well represented in a case concerning a German national's application against the United Kingdom. Mr. Soering was to be extradited to the United States for the murder of his girlfriend's parents. He committed the offense at the age of 18 and was considered to have a substantially impaired mental responsibility. In the case brought against UK, he alleged that his extradition would breach Article 3 of the European Convention which prohibits torture or inhuman or degrading treatment of punishment.

He reached this conclusion because his extradition could mean being sentenced to death in Virginia and the fore exposed to inhumane conditions of being on death row. The European Court of Human Rights in unanimity found that:

"... having regard to the very long period of time spent on death row in such extreme conditions, with the ever present and mounting anguish of awaiting execution of the death penalty, and to the personal circumstances of the applicant, especially his age and mental state at the time of the offence, the applicant's extradition to the United States would expose him to a real risk of treatment going beyond the threshold set by Article 3...... Accordingly, the Secretary of State's decision to extradite the applicant to the United States would, if implemented, give rise to a breach of Article 3.[3]

The decision of the court reaffirm the importance of the individual rights guaranteed under Article 3 despite the crime committed by Mr Soering. Like in many other cases(i.e., *the Tyrer case, the Krocher and Muller case, B .v. the United Kingdom* and *the M. Chartier case*), the European Commission and the Court have contributed tremendously to the process of enforcement. The Council of Europe created a body of international inspection charged with visiting the territory of European states in an attempt to satisfying itself whether torture and violation of human rights has taken place.

The European Commission example shows how successful a commitment to the protection of human rights among member states could be, especially with the existence of an international tribunal like the European Court. The situation is also made possible by the prevailing political conditions characterized by constitutional democracies which permits the individual the potential to seek redress not only in the local courts but in an international tribunal.

On the contrary the *Forti* v. *Suarez-Mason* case shows how domestic courts can act as a substitute for absent international machinery. These domestic courts " turn themselves into the arm of the law"[4] if not only to issue penal sanction but to at least award compensation for damages and denounce the misdeed of governments and individuals in a public forum. The domestic courts are able to play this important roles because they exist within a democratic society. Under authoritarian governments, it is extremely unlikely that judges will have the independence and probably the audacity to rule against the government without being subjected to the same level of repression that most of the society exist under.

There are three different levels for the protection of human rights. The first and the most important is within the primary society within which the individual lives. A constitutional democracy is good for individual freedom. Governments can improve their human rights records by initiating domestic reforms that demonstrate adherence to human rights norms.

At the second level, a government and a group of governments can enforce at regional levels punitive actions against a state violating human rights norms . And at the third level, the international community can take punitive actions against any state violating any international human rights regimes, through the use of sanctions and possibly military force.

As human rights evolve over time, it continuously, through series of international instruments binds all states in the world, to both moral and political obligations constitutive of natural- law principles. It also bind those states that are explicitly signatories to the agreements, under which they have no way out. There should be no flexibility in terms of implementation and punitive measures against violators of human rights. The international community cannot afford to be selective in its actions concerning human rights application. The nature of government, the strategic importance of the state in question and the historical relationship between such a state and other major powers should not be allowed to influence actions in response to human rights violations.

The international community and especially the United Nations cannot afford to ignore violations of human rights in many part of the world because such a propensity can threaten international peace and security. There should be a preventive mechanism for detecting violation and for initiating rapid response to situations like those we saw in Bosnia and Rwanda. Extensive provision should be made to assist and coordinate humanitarian efforts and monitoring human rights violations. The world community is in dare need of an effective international enforcement mechanism, such as an international court to support the United Nations .

ENDNOTES

Chapter 1

1. M. Moskowitz, *The Politics and dynamics of Human Rights*,(1968)(London: Stevens).
   see also, M.S. Mcdougal, H.D. Lasswell and Lung-Chu Chen (ed.), *Human rights and World Public order*, (New Haven: Yale Univ. Press (1980).
2. M.S. Mcdougal, et al, Human Rights and World Public order, ibid. p. 68.
3. See Cranston, *What are Human Rights?* (1973)(New Haven: Yale University Press), also R. Bilder, *Rethinking International Human Rights: Some Basic Questions* (1969)(Univ. Wiscon. Press)
4. See J. Carter, *Law: Its origin, growth and function*, (1907)(Oxford: OUP) see also H. Maine, *Ancient Law*,(1963)(Laud: Dent), R. Pound, *Interpretations of Legal History* (1923)(Cambridge: CUP.)and P. Vinogradoff, *Outlines of Historical Jurisprudence* (1920-22) (London: OUP).
5. Mcdougal et al, Human Rights and World Public order,(op. cit.) p. 71.
6. See P. Drost, *Human Rights as legal Rights*, (1951)(London: Stevens) and also H. Lauterpacht, *International Law and Human* (1950) (London: Stevens)
7. See J. Austin, *The Province of Jurisprudence Determined and Uses of the Study of Jurisprudence* (1954) (Glassgow: Collins/ Fontana);H. Hart, *The Concept of Law*, (1961) (Oxford: Clarendon Press)and H. Kelsen, *General Theory of Law and State* (1945)(Cambridge, MA: Harvard Univ. Press).
8. Chalidze, *To defend those rights: Human Rights and the Soviet Union* (1974)(London: Collins & Harvey)p. 3-49.

9. J. Hazard, *Communists and their Law: A search for the common core of the legal systems of the Marxian Socialist States* (1969)(Cambridge: CUP) p.139.
10. Danelski, "A Behavioural Conception of Human Rights ", 3 *Law In Transition*, Q63 (1966) and Feeley, " The Concept of Laws in Social Science: A Critique and Notes On An Expanded view", *10 Law & Society Review*, (1976).

Chapter 2

1. Charles E. Wyzanski, (jr)(1979), The Philosophical Background of the Doctrine of Human right in A.H. Henkin (ed.) Human Dignity: The Internationalization of Human Right (New York: Aspen Institute for Humanistic Studies/ Oceana Publi, 1979)
2. John Locke, Two Treatises of Civil Government (2nd ed.) Peter Laslett (ed), (N.Y.: Cambridge Univ. Press, 1960).
3. Robert Nozick,(1974) Anarchy State and Utopia (Oxford: Basic Books Inc., 1974), p. 10.
4. Robert Nozick, Anarchy State and Utopia, p.12. see also, Giereke Otto, Natural Law and The Theory of Society, 1560 - 1800 (Cambridge: CUP, 1934); H. Ronald," Hayek's Concept of Freedom: A Critique", *New Individualist Reviews*, (April 1961), p.28-31; H.L.A. Hart, "Are there any Natural Rights?," *Philosophical Review*, 64 (1955) p. 175-91, Hayek F.A., *The Constitution of Liberty*, (Chicago, Univ. of Chicago Press,1960); Nelson Leonard, *System of Ethics*, (New Haven, CT: Yale Univ. Press, 1956); Rousseau J.J. *The Social contract*,(London, Everyone's library, 1917); Tawaey R.H. *Equality*, (London: Allen and Unwin, 1938), and Tucket Benjamin, *Individual liberty* (N.Y.: Vanguard Press, 1926).
5. Jeremy Waldron (ed.), Theories of Rights, (London: OUP, 1984).
6. See G.E.M. Anscombe, "Modern Moral Philosophy" in her collection, Ethnic, Religion and Politics, *Collected Philosophical Papers* Vol. III(Oxford: OUP, 1981),p.13 and p. 40.
7. Robert Nozick, *op cit.*, p. 28.
8. See Kant's Political writings (ed.) H. Reiss, (Cambridge, CUP 1970)p.79, and Peter Laslett (ed), John Locke, Two Treatises of Civil Government (Cambridge: CUP, 1960)p. II, chapters 9 and 11.

9. See Margaret Macdonald, "Natural Rights" in Jeremy Waldron (ed.).*op. cit.*

10. John Finnis, *Natural law and Natural Rights*, (Oxford: Clarendon Press, 1972), p. 250.

11. Beryl Harold Levy, *Making Human Rights more definite and effective.* (London: Transition.1985)

12. See Encycl. Pacem in Terries, of John XXIII (American Press ed., 1963), p. 28-33.

13. Alejo de Cervera, "Natural Law Restated. An analysis of liberty." E.H. Pollack (ed) *What are Human Rights?* Buffalo, N.Y.: Jay Stewart Publication Inc., 1971).

14. Pacem in Terries (Encycl. (S 29 of 10).

15. Note. Article 29, the Universal Declaration of Human Rights, adopted by the UNGA on December 10th, 1948.

16. Signed on October 19th, 1961, by the members of the Council of Europe, (European Treaty Series No.35)(European Commission).

17. See Hohfeld, fundamental legal conceptions as applied in judicial reasoning (1923)(Westport: CT: Greenwood/YUP), p. 38. see also, D.J. Harris (1991), Cases and Materials On International Law. 4th. edition (London, England: Sweet and Maxwell).

18. F.E. Dowrick, (ed.), Human Rights :Problems, Perspectives and Texts (Westmead, England: Saxon House, 1979).

19. See also Salmont J. *Jurisprudence*, 2nd ed. (1966)(London: Sweet & Marxwell); Hohfeld(1923) *op cit.*; H.L.A. Hart, "Definition and Theory In Jurisprudence" *70 Law Quarterly Review* (1954), p. 37- 49.

20. A.J.M. Milne, "The idea of Human rights: A Critical inquiry," in F.E. Dowrick (ed.).op. cit.

21. D. Raphael, *Moral Judgement* (1955).(London: Allen & Unwin)

22. R.M. Dworkin, *Taking rights seriously* (London: Duckworth 1977), p. 91.

23. R.M. Dworkin, *Taking rights seriously*, p. 269. op. cit.

24. Dworkin, (1977) 191 - But Dworkin continues 'I must not overstate the point. Someone who claims that citizens have a right against the Government need not go so far as to say that the state is never justified in overriding that right. He might say, for example, that although citizens have a right to free speech, the Government may override that right when necessary to protect others or to prevent catastrophe or even to obtain a clear and major public benefit (though if he acknowledge this last as a

possible justification, he would be treating the right in question as not among the most important or fundamental).

25. John Finnis (1982) *Natural Law and Natural Rights*.(Oxford: Clarendon Press)

26. J. Waldron, Theories of Rights,(op. cit.) p. 12.

27. R. Giffrey, *Interest and Rights: The Case Against the Annuals* (Oxford, Clarendon)(1980).It should be borne in mind that the interest theorists do not define rights in terms of a concept that it is itself lucid and uncontestable, rather what they have done is to indicate how controversies about rights lock into wider framework of controversies about interest. See also Dworkin, *Taking Rights Seriously* (London: Duckworth, 1978)(rev. edition) p.169.

28. Leyman E. Allen, "Right$_1$, Right$_2$, Rights$_3$, Rights$_4$ - And how about Right," in E.H. Pollack (ed.) op cit.

29. Wesley N. Honfeld, "Fundamental Legal Conception as Applied in Judicial Reasoning," 23 *Yale L.J.* 16, 29 1913.
    See also Felix S. Cohen," Transcendental Nonsense and the Functional Approach," 35 *Colum. L. Review* (1935) 809, 824-829. See Honfeld article i.e. notes 32, 34, 36a, 65 and 96.

30. See Honfeld, "Fundamental Legal Conception as Applied in Judicial Reasoning," Analysis of legal doctrine: The normative Structure of Positive law," 53 *IOWA L. Rev* (1968), p. 1209, 1268.

31. Jeremy Waldron, Theories of Rights,(op. cit.)
    See also The Declaration of the Rights of Man and the citizen (French National Assembly 27 Aug, 1789), Article 11.

32. See Richard Tuck, *Natural Rights theories: their Origins and Development* (Cambridge: CUP 1979); H. Kelsen, Pure Theory of Law (Berkeley, Univ. of California Press,1970)p.125.

33. See Carl Friedrich, "Rights, Liberties, Freedoms: A Reappraisal," *American Political Science review*, 57 (1963), p. 844, H.J. McCloskey, Moral Rights and Animals *Inquiry* 22 (1979), p. 43-4, 48-9.

34. See W.T. Blackstone, "Equality and Human Rights." *The Monist* 52, (1968), p. 626-7.

35. See Waldron, Theories of Rights,(op. cit.) and also Simon Blackburn, "Rule-Following and Moral Realism" in Wittgenstein, *To follow a rule,* (London: S. Holtzman & C. Leich, 1981), p. 174.

36. See also H.L.A. Hart's "Definition and Theory in Jurisprudence" *Law Quarterly Review* 70 (1954); D.M. MacCormic, "Rights in legislation" *Law, morality and society*, Essays in Honour of H.L.A. Hart (Oxford: OUP, 1977), p. 188-91.

    - For more on different senses of rights - see J. Feinberg *Social Philosophy*, (Englewood Cliffs, N.J: Prentice Hall 1973 chap. 4).

    - For interaction between privileges and claims - rights, see H.L.A. Hart, "Bentham on legal rights" in Oxford Essays in Jurisprudence (2nd series) A.W.B. Simpson (ed) (Oxford, OUP 1977), p. 175-6; Thomas Hobbes, *Leviathan* (1651), chap. 14; Hobbes, De Cive or The citizen (ed.), Sterling Lamprecht (N.Y:Apple-Century-Crofts,1949); G.W. Paton, A Textbook On Jurisprudence (4th.ed.) (Oxford: Claredon Press, 1972)p.293; J. Waldron and W. Galstron in *Ethics* 93 (1983), p. 320-7; Joel Feinberg, Rights, Justice and the Bounds of liberty (Princeton: Princeton Univ. Press. 1980), chap. 6-7; A.I. Melden, Rights and Persons (Oxford: Blackwell, 1977); V. Hakkar, "The Nature of Rights," *Activ fur Recht und sozial philosophie* 64(1978), p. 183; David Lyons 'Rights, Claimants and Beneficiaries," *American Philosophical Quarterly* 6,(1969),esp. p. 75-80.

37. Carl Wellman, "A new Conception of Human Rights" in E. Kamenka & A.E.S. Tay(ed.), *Human Rights* (London: Edward Arnold,1978), see also the discussion between M. Cranston and D.D. Raphael in *Political Theory and the Rights of Man* (London: Macmillian, 1967) & T.D. Campbell, The Left and Rights (London: Allen & Unwin 1983), chaps.6 & 9.

Chapter 3

1. See E.H. Pollack, *Human Rights (Aminta phil 1)* (Buffalo N.Y. Jay Steward Publication Inc., 1971). In his introduction, some distinctive nature of each of the family of rights are given i.e. legal - element of human enactment (adding the typical sanction of the law), moral - ethical grounding with the good and sometimes obligation are given central position, natural rights - after being classified as moral rights have right remain relative to all.

2. See Kai Neiben, "Scepticism and Human Rights," *The Monist* Vol. 52, no. 4 of 1968, p. 594 and M. Mcdonald, "Natural Rights" *Proceedings of the Aristotelian society* vol. 47 (1947-48), p. 225-50.

3. See W.T. Blackstone "Equality and Human Rights" *The Monist*, vol. 52, No. 4 Oct. 1968.

4. See W. Frankea's "Recent conceptions of morality," W.D. Falk "Morality, Self and Others" both in *Morality and the language of Conduct*, edited by Hector N. Castageda and George Nakhnikian (Detroit: Wayne State Univ. Press 1965).

5. See Martin Golding's (ed.) *The Nature of Law* (1966), for the discussion of the nature of law and the relationship between law and morality. Also Hart-Fulkes debate:-H.L.A. Hart "Positivism and the separation of law and morality" and Lon Fuller "positivism and fidelity to Law a reply to Professor Hart" both in *Harvard Law Review* (1958).

6. W.T. Blackstone, "The justification of Human Rights" in A.H. Henkin (ed.) *Human Dignity: The Internationalization of Human Rights* (New York, AIHS/Oceania P. Inc. & S&N 1979), p. 3.

7. E.H. Pollack, *Human Rights*.(Op. cit.). See also Paul Ellen Frankel (1984), *Human Rights*(Bowling Green State Univ. Press)

8. W.T. Blackstone, in E.H. Pollack (ed.) *Human Rights*.

9. F.E. Dowrick (ed.) (1979), Human Rights :Problems, perspectives and Texts. (op. cit.)

10. James F. Doyle "Personal claims, Human Rights and Social Justice," in E.H. Pollack (ed.) op. cit.

11. J.E.S. Fawcett, "The International protection of Human Rights" in D.D. Raphael (ed.) Political Theory and The Rights of Man (London: Macmillan 1967), p. 125.

12. Lauterpacht, "International Law and Human Rights" (N.Y.: Praeger 1950), p. 74, see also, Joel Feinberg, "Duties, Rights and Claims *American Philosophical Quarterly* 3 (April 1966), p. 143.

13. See J.F. Doyle, op cit.: Brian Barry, *Political arguments* (London: Routledge and Kegan Paul 9165);A.M. Honore "Social Justice" in R.S. Summers (ed.) *Essays in legal philosophy* (Oxford: Basil Blackwell, 1968); David Braybok, *Three tests for Democracy: Personal Rights, Human Welfare, Collective Preferences* (N.Y: Random House, 1968),p. 46; Bernard Mays "What are Human Rights?" in D.D. Raphael (ed.) *op cit.* and J.E.S. Fawcett, "The Role of the United Nations in the Protection of Human Rights - Is it Misconceived?" in Asbjorn Eide and August Shou (ed.), *International Protection of Human Rights* (N.Y: Inter-Science Publishers 1968), p. 95-101.

13.2   R.J. Vincent, *Human Rights and International Relations* (Cambridge, England: Cambridge Univ. Press 1988), p. 49.

14. See F.E. Dowrick, Human Rights; Jacobs (F.G.) *The European Convention on Human Rights* (1975)(Oxford: Clarendon Press) part III and A.H. Robertson *Human Rights In Europe.* (2nd ed.) (1977)(Manchester: Manchester Univ. Press), p. 110-7.

Chapter 4

1. M. Mascowitz "Implementing Human Rights" in B.G. Ramcharan (ed.) *Human Rights: Thirty Years After the Universal Declaration* (The Hague: Martinus Nijhoff, 1979), p. 111.

2. See J.P. Humphrey "The Universal Declaration of Human Rights: Its history, Impact and Juridical character" in B.H. Ramcharan (ed.) Human Rights; also Humphrey "The UN Charter and the Universal Declaration of Human Rights" in Luard (ed.) *The International Protection of Human Rights* (London: Thames & Hudson, 1967), p. 40.

3. Ecosoc, Res 1/5 of 16 Feb. 1946.

4. Joel Feinberg *Social Philosophy* (Englewood-Cliffs, NJ: Prentice Hall 1973) p. 67.

5. J. Humphrey, "The Universal Declaration of Human Rights: Its History, Impacts, and juridical character." Op. cit.

6. See the preamble of this Convention.

7. See "United Nations Action in the field of Human Rights" UN Publication ST/HR/2 (and many other documents of the UN Commission on Human Rights).

8. See Sir Humphrey Waldrock, 106 *Receuil des Cours* (1962), p. 198.

9. J. Humphrey "The Universal Declaration of Human Rights." op. cit.

10. See *The Continental Shelf Cases* I.C.J. Reports 1969, p. 3 (p. 44).

11. F.E. Dowrick (ed.) *Human Rights.* Op. cit.

12. F.E. Dowrick (ed.) *Human Rights.* Ibid.

13. See the preamble and Article 2 of the Universal Declaration, United Nations.

Chapter 5

1. H.G. Espiell "The evolving concept of Human Rights: Western, Socialist and Third World approaches" in B.G. Ramcharan (ed.) *Human Rights: Thirty Years after the Universal Declaration* (The Hague: Martinus Nijhoff, 1979).
2. B. Ramcharan, *Human Rights in the Third World* (Background Paper, Division of Human Rights UN 1977), p. 10.
3. Proclamation of Teheran par. 12, 13 and 14.
4. References to the UN Universal Declaration of Human Rights in several African constitutions such as those of Guinea 1958, Mali 1960, Niger 1960, Gabon 1961, Mauritania 1961, Burundi 1962, Somali 1960, Algeria 1963, Republic of Congo 1963, Senegal 1963, Togo 1963, Zaire 1967, Dahomey (Benin) 1970, Ruwanda 1962 and Equatorial Africa (1968) see also O. Okott- Ogendo "National Implementation of International Responsibility: Some Thoughts on Human Rights in Africa" *East Africa Law Journal* vol. 10 no. 1 1974, p. 14.
5. T.O. Elias "The New Constitution of Nigeria and the Protection of Human Rights and Fundamental Freedoms" *The Judicial Review 1960*, Vol. II p. 39-46.
    See also Jean-Flarien Lalive, forward to the African Conference on the Rule of Law, Lagos, Nigeria, 3-7 Jan. 1961. A report on the Proceeding of the Conference, *International Commission of Jurist*, Geneva, 1961, p. 6 (Lalive was then the Secretary-General of the International Commission of Jurists) and Keba M'baye, "Human rights in Africa" in Karel Vasaks (ed.) *The International Dimensions of Human Rights* (ed.) Karel Vasaks (Vol. 2)(Westport, CT: Greenwood Press & Paris: UNESCO Press 1982), p. 583.
6. Preamble (par. 1 & 2) OAU Charter, May 1963. See also Osite Eze, "Prospect for the Inter-Protection of Human Rights in Africa", *The African Review* Vol. 4 No. 1 1974; B. Ndiaie, "The   Place of Human Rights in the Charter of the OAU" K. Vasaks (ed.) *International Dimensions of Human Rights*, B.O. Okere, "The Protection of Human Rights in Africa and the African Charter of Human and People's Rights: A Comparative Analysis with the European and American Systems" *Human Rights quarterly* Vol. 6, No. 2 1984, p. 141-199; *Human Rights in a one-party-State* (London: International Commission of Jurists/ Search Press.

Sept. 1976); Richard Gittleman, "The African Charter on Human   and People's Rights: A legal analysis *Virginia Journal of International Law*, vol. 22, 1981-82, p. 667-714.

7. J. Salmon "Rapport sur le droit de peuples a disposer d'eux memes" *Annales de la faculte de droit des sciences economiques de Reims* 1974 (Paris: ASER)p.268.

8. E.G. Bello "Human Rights: The Rule of Law in Africa" *I & CLQ* vol. 30, 1981, p. 628-637.

9. E.G. Bello *The African Charter on Human and People's Rights - a legal analysis* (Hague: Martinus Nijhoff Publ.,1985).

10. See Rhode Howard, "The full-belly thesis: should Economic rights take priority over civil and Political Rights? A discussion from sub Saharan Africa (Development studies Program, University of Toronto. Working Paper no. A3 April 1983); Reginald Green, "Basic Human Rights/Needs. Some Problems of categorical Translation and Unification" *The Review* (International Commission of Jurists No. 24-27, 1980- 81, p. 55).

11. Henry Shue, *Basic Rights: Subsistence, Affluence and US foreign Policy* (Princeton, NJ: PUP 1980), Chap. 1.

12. Sylvia Ann Hawlett, "Human Rights and Economic Realities: Trade offs in Historical Perspectives" *Political Science Quarterly* Vol. 94, No. 3 Fall 1979, p. 412. See also R.S. Goldstein, "Political Repression and political development: The 'Human Right' issue in 19th Century Europe" in R.F. Tomasson (ed.) *Comparative Social Research* vol. 4, (Greenwich, CT., Joi Press 1981), p. 144 and F.M. Hayward "Political Participation and its role in Development: Some observations drawn from the African Context" *Journal of developing Areas*. Vol. 7 July 1973, p. 610.

13. R.M. Mach, "Does Democracy Hinder Economic Development in late comer Developing Nations?" in R.F. Tomasson (ed.) *Comparative Social Research*. Vol. 4. 1981

14. Paul Strecten and S.J. Burki, Basic Needs: Some issues" *World Development*, vol. 6, No. 3 1978, p. 411.

15. O. Aluko, "The Organization of African Unity and Human Rights" *The Round Table* Vol. 283, July 1981, p. 237.

16. Van Boven, "The right to Development and Human Rights" *The Review* (of the International Commission of Jurists),p. 49, 1982.

17. See Blackstone, "Equality and Human Rights" *The Monist* Vol. 52, No. 4 Oct. 1968, p. 627-28; Herbert Morris, "Persons and Punishment" *The*

Monist Vol. 52, No. 4 Oct. 1968, p. 495-497; Frederick Olafson "Essence and concept in Natural Law theory" in *Law and Philosophy* (ed.) Sidney Hook (N.Y.OUP. 1964), p. 239 and Jacques Maritain, *The rights of Man and Natural Law* (London Longman 1943), p. 59.

18. R.J. Vincent *Human Rights and International Relations* (Cambridge: CUP, 1988), p. 13.

Chapter 6

1. H.G. Espielle, "The evolving concept of Human Rights" in B.G. Ramcharan (ed) *Human Rights*, Op. cit. p. 64.
2. J. Freymond, "Human Rights and Foreign Policy" in B.G. Ramcharan (ed.) *Human Rights*, Op. cit. p. 69.
3. J. Freymond "Human Rights and Foreign Policy", Ibid. p. 79.
3.2 Ed. Sparer, "Fundamental Human Rights, legal entitlement and Social struggle" *Stanord Law Review* Jan. 1984 Vol. 36, No. 1 & 2.
3.3 Ibid.
4. E.H. Pollack (ed.) *Human Rights*, Op. cit. p. 3.
5. E.H. Pollack (ed.) *Human Rights*, op. cit. p. 5.
6. Elaine Pagels, "The roots and origins of Human Rights" in A.H. Henkim (ed.) *Human Dignity*, op. cit. p. 2.
7. Elaine Pagels, "The roots and origins of Human Rights." op. cit.
8. See Elaine Pagels. ibid.
9. The Holy Bible (Gideons International).
10. The Holy Koran.
11. See Isaiah Berlin "Two concepts of liberty" in Four essays on liberty, (Oxford: OUP 1969), p. 129; Judaism and Human Rights in *Judaism: A Quarterly Journal of Jewish Life and thought*, Vol. 25, No. 4 1976, p. 435; W.H.C. *Frend Martyrdom and Persecution in the Early Church* (Oxford: OUP, 1965) and Tor Andrace, *Mohammed, the man and his faith*, (London: Harper and Row, 1960), p. 75.

Chapter 7

1. Kennedy, Paul (1987), The Rise and Fall of the Great Powers (New York: Random House), See also William F. Felice (1996), "The Case for Collective Human Rights: The Reality of Group Suffering", *Ethics and*

International Affairs. Vol. 10.1996.; Goldstein, J.S.(1988), Long Cycle: Prosperity and War In Modern Age(New Haven, CT: Yale University Press); Levy J.S.(1992), "The Causes of War: Contending Theories" in Charles W. Kegley Jr and Eugene R. WittKopf (ed.)(1992), The Global Agenda (3rd. Edition)(New York: McGraw-Hill) and Modelski G. and Thompson W.R. 1989)," Long Cycles and Global War" in Manus I and Midlarsky (ed.) (1989) Handbook of War Studies (Boston: Unwin Hyman)

2. Charles W. Kegley Jr. and Eugene R. Wittkopf (1993), World Politics: Trend and Transformation(New York: St Martin's Press)p.87.
3. Oberdorfer, D.(1991),The Turn: From Cold War to a New Era(New York: Poseidon).

Chapter 8

1. Richard J. Stoll & Michael D. Ward (1989), Power In World Politics (Boulder, Colorado: Lynne Rienner).p.130
2. Jack Donnelly (1991), "Progress In Human Rights" in Emanuel Adler and Beverly Crawford (1991), Progress In Post War International Relations (New York: Columbia University Press)
3. Amnesty International Report(1994) p.33-34
    See also, EveryOne's United Nations (New York: UN Department of Public Information, 1986)p 304-307.
4. Shashi Tharoor (1996) " The Future of Peacekeeping" in Witman, Jim and Pocock, David (ed.)(1996) After Rwanda: The Coordination of United Nations Humanitarian Assistance (New York: St Martin's Press)p.18
5. Antonio Cassese(1990) Human Rights In a Changing World (Philadelphia, PA: Temple University Press)p.85
6. Ibid. p.85
7. See also Hafbauer, G.C and Scholt, J.J.(1985), Economic Sanction Reconsidered: History and Current Policy(Washington D.C: Institute of International Economic); Daoudi, M.S and Dajami, M.S.(1983), Economic Sanction: Idea and Experience London: Routhledge and Kegan Paul); Dewey John(1930)"Are Sanctions Necessary to International Organization" *Series 1930-31, no:1 pamphlet No:82, New York Foreign policy Association, June 1932.;*Hander Ali Khan(1989)The Political

Economy of Sanction Against Apartheid(boulder, Colorado: Lynne Rienner Publ.)

7a. Woodrow Wilson's Case for the League of Nations, compiled with his approval by Hamilton Foley(1923),(Princeton, NJ: Princeton University Press)p.71-72.

8. A dictionary of International Law (Progress Publishers, Moscow 1982).

9. H. Kelsen. The law of *the United Nations* [London: Stevens & Sons Ltd, 1954 p 197.

9a. ibid

10. Article 2, paragraph 2, UN Charter.

11. Article 25, UN Charter.

12. Article 94, paragraph 1, UN Charter.

13. A Dictionary of International Law.

14. L.B.Sohn, "Expulsion or forced Withdrawal from an International Organisation", *HLR* Vol. 77, No 8, June 1964.

15. H. Kelsen, The Law of the United Nations, p197.

16. H. Kelsen, The Law of the UN.

17. Article 16, paragraph 4 of the Covenant of the League of Nations.

18. League of Nations, Doc No A.C.13.

19. League of Nations Official Record, 20th Ass. Plenary, 14, 16-17 (1939).

20. L.N. Official Journal, 20th Ass. 506 (1959).

21. Louis B. Sohn, "Expulsion or forced Withdrawal from an International Organisation". op. cit.

22. Jenks, "Expulsion from the League of Nations" 16 BYIL 155, 156, (1935).(British Year of International Law)

23. L.N. off J. 20th Ass 387 - 388 (1939).

24. See League of Nations, Reports and Resolutions on Article 16, 18 - 19, 60, 70; L.N. Doc. No A 14.1927.V; L.N. Pub. No V. Legal 1927. V.14.

25. Kelsen, Legal Technic in International law: A textual critique of the League's Covenant, (1939), p 67, 78, 145-46 & 150.

26. Ray, Commentaire du Pacte de la Societe des Nations (1930) p 273 - 74, 535.

27. Schucking & Wehberg, Die satzung des Volkerbundes (1931 3rd ed.) p.582-83 (cited in L.B. Sohn).

28. Schucking & Wehberg, Die satzung des Volkerbundes (1924 2nd ed.)p. 626.

29. League of Nations Off Rec, 20th Ass., Plenary 53 (1939) - In the other half of the resolution, relating to assistance to Finland, the Assembly expressed the view that the Soviet Union "has failed to observe not only its special political agreements with Finland, but also Article 12 of the Covenant of the League of Nations and the Pact of Paris", and made reference to the illegal Soviet denunciation of the non aggression Treaty with Finland, cited in L.B. Sohn "Expulsion or forced Withdrawal from an International Organisation" Harvard Law Review Vol. 77, No 8, 1964, p 1393.

30. L.B. Sohn, "Expulsion or forced withdrawal p.1394.

31. Elea, Le principe de l'unanimite dans la Societe des Nations, (1935)(cited in L.B. Sohn) p35.

32 Balossini, Le declin de la Societe des Nations la perte de la qualite de membre de la S.D.N. (Le cas de l'U.R.S.S. et de la France) 1945, p43 - 44.

33. L.B. Sohn, *op cit*

34. Goodrich B. Hambro, Charter of the United Nations: Commentary & Documents (1949 2nd ed.) p 140 - 41.

35. 7 UN Conf Int'l Org. Docs (1945) p330 - 31.

36. ibid

37. L.B. Sohn, *op cit*, p 1401.

38. OJO B.A., United Nations and Sanctions: A study of Transnational Corporations and effective sanction against Apartheid [MSc Thesis Univ of Ife .Ile-Ife, Nigeria.1986) p4.

39. Wilmot P.F., Apartheid and African Liberation, [Ile-Ife University of Ife. Press. Ile-Ife. Nigeria 19801 p (viii).

40. UN Council for Namibia: Report to the General Assembly. Doc. 4/ 9024.

41. Article 55 (c) of the UN Charter.

42. Article 39 of the Charter [see also Articles 41, 42, 5 & 6 for more on UN Sanction]. See K. Gyeke Dako, Economic Sanctions Under the United Nations (Accra-Tema, Ghana Publ. Corp. 1973) p.23.

43. Resolution 176 (xvii) 6 Nov 1962.

44. UNSO Resolution 282, July 1970.

45. Colin Legum, "International Rivalries in the Southern African Conflict", in G. Carter & P. O'Meara, eds. South Africa: The Continuing Crisis (London: Macmillan Press ltd 1979) p.6.

46. F.S. Northedge, The International Political System (London: Faber and Faber, 1976) p27.

47 International Court of Justice (ICJ) Report 1962, p168.

48. ICAO Assembly Proceeding 1st Session 237 (ICAO Doc 7325 - C/852 [19521).

49. UN Gen. Ass. Off. Rec. 5th Session. Supp. No 20, at 16/A/1775 [19501

50. 2 U.N.T.S. 40 (1947).

51. See IMF Summary Proceedings, Annual Meeting 1954, p24-25.

52. 2 U.N.T.S. 172 (1947).

53. IBRD, Summary Proceedings Annual Meeting 1953, p24-25.

54. 4 U.N.T.S. 280 (1947).

55. 289 U.N.T.S. 54 (1958).

56. UN ECOSOC Council Off. Rec. 34th Session, Supp. No 10 p.39-41 [E/35861 1962.

57. Esc Rec 974 Div (2) July 30 1963, 36 ESCOR Supp. No I p.4 E/3816.

58. Statute of the Council of Europe, May 5, 1949, Art 3.

59. Charter of the Organisation of American States, April 30, 1948, Article 25, 119 U.N.T.S. 60 (1952).

60. L.B. Sohn, *op cit.* p 1418.

61. E. Oseike "Sanction in International Law. The Constitution of International Organisations" NILR 1984.(Nigerian International Law Review)

62. Friedman, "General Course of Public International Law". *Hague Recueil* (1969) p 115 - 116.

Chapter 9

1. Preamble, Universal Declaration of Human Rights, United Nations. 1948.

2. A.J.M. Milne (1986), Human Rights and Human Diversity: An Essay In The Philosophy of Human Rights (Albany, NY: SUNY Press)p. 2

3. ibid, p.5

Chapter 10

1. Ranney Austin (1990), Governing: An Introduction to Political Science(Englewood Cliff, NJ: Prentice Hall) p. 385.

2. James Turner Johnson(1990), "Is Democracy An Ethical Standard" *Ethics and International Affairs* Vol. 4, 1990.

3. Soering Case, 7 July 1989, European Court of Human Rights, Series A, Vol. 16, p.357.
4. Antonio Cassesse (1990), Human Rights In a Changing World (Philadelphia, PA: Temple University Press) p.102.

BIBLIOGRAPHY

The Bibliography is divided into two:
A:(i) Books and (ii) Articles
B: *Official* documents

- United Nations Publications

- International Labour Organizations Documents

- Other Specialized Agencies - i.e. UNESCO etc.

- European Community Documents on Human Rights

- Organization of African Unity

- Organization of American States

A(I): BOOKS

ALSTON, P. "Development and the rule of law: prevention versus cure as a human rights strategy" in *Development, Human Rights and the Rule of Law*, Report of a Conference held in The Hague on 27th April - 1st May 1981 (Oxford: Pergamon Pres, 1981)

ALSTON, P. & TOMASKEVI K. (eds.), The Right to food (The Hague: Martinus Nijhoff), 1984).

ASBJORN EIDE & A. SCHOU (eds.), International Protection of Human Rights (Stockholm/NY: InterScience Pbl.1968).

ARAT, Zehra. F.(1991), Democracy and Human Rights In Developing Countries(Boulder, CO: Lynne Rienner Publ.)

ARENS R. (ed.), Genocide in Paraguay (Philadelphia, PA: Temple UP Press 1976).

B.A. ABDOUL, KEFFI, BRUNO, SAALI, FETHI, L'Organization de l'Unite Africaine de la Charte d'Addis Abeba a la Convention des droit de d'Homme et des Peuples (Sept. 1984, Chateau Gonher).

BEDJAO M., Towards a New International Economic Order (Paris: UNESCO, 1979).

BELLO, E.G., The African Charter on Human and Peoples Rights, (London: Martinus. N 1985).

BIRYUKOVA, A., Equal Rights and Equal Opportunities (Moscow: Profizdat Publishers, 1985).

CASSESE, A. & JOUVE, E., (eds) Pur un Droit des Peuples Essais sur la Declaration d'Alger (Paris: Berger Levrault, 1978).

CASSIN R., De la place aux devoirs de l'individu dans la Declaration Universelle des Droit de l'Homme in Melanges offerts a Polys Mochnus (Paris: Edition A Pedone 1968).

CHAUDHURI K., Genocide in Bangladesh (Bombay: Orient-Longman, 1972).

CRAWFORD, J., (ed.) The Rights of Peoples (Oxford: Clarendon Press, 1988).

- The Creation of States in International Law (Oxford: Clarendon Press, 1979).

CHOMSKY, N. & HERMAN, E.S., The Political Economy of Human Rights (2 vol.), Boston,MA: Southend Press 1979.

CRISTESCU, A., The Right to Self-Determination. Historical and Current Development on the Basis of United Nations Instruments (UN Doc e/CN 4/sub 2/404/Rev 1, 1981).

CHAND, H., Fundamental Rights in Nigeria (Jos, Nigeria:UJP,1980). Council of Europe, Human Rights in International Law, Basic Texts, Directorate of Human Rights, Strasbourg, 1985.

- The Protection of Human Rights in Europe, Strasbourg 1981.

CONE, B., & HARRIS J., (eds.) Human Rights in Africa (Wellington, N.Z: Africa Information Centre 1983).

DAES E. IA 'Protection of minorities under the International Bill of Rights and the Genocide Convention', in Xenon, Festschrift fur Pan J. Zepos (Athens: Katsikalis Verlag,1973).

DAKO, K.G (1973), Economic Sanctions Under the United Nations (Accra Tema, Ghana: Ghana Publ. Corp. 1973)

DEWAR, J., Nuclear Weapons, the Peace Movement and the Law (Basingstoke: Macmillan 1986).

DOKU, E.F.T., The International Protection of Human Rights in African, M.S.C. (Thesis) Institute of Social Studies, The Hague, Sept., 1978).

DROST, P.N., Human Rights as Legal Rights, the Realization of Individual Human Rights in Positive International Law (Leinden/New York: A.W. Sijthoff Vitjeversmy, 1951).

DWORKIN, R., Taking Rights Seriously (London: Clarendon 1978).

DUPUY, R.J., (ed.) The Right to Development at the Internation level, (Alphen aan den Rijn: Sijthoff and Noordhoff, 1980).

 - L'Avenir du Droit International de l'Environment. Colloque de l'Academie de Droit International de la Haye (Dordrecht: Martinus Nijhoff, 1985).

DUFFET, J., (ed.) Against the Crime of Silence: Proceedings of the International War Crimes Tribunal (NY: Simon and Schuster, 1970).

ELIAS, T.O., Human Rights and the Developing Countries: New Horizons in International Law (The Hague: Sijthoff and Nordhoff 1979).

EWING, D.W., Freedom Inside the Organization: Bringing of Civil Liberties to the Working Place (1977).

EZEJIOFOR, G., African Convention of Human Rights (London: Butterworths, 1964).

FALK, R.A., The Status of Law in International Society (Princeton: Princeton U. Press, 1970).

 - Human Right and State Sovereignty (N.Y.: Holmes & Meier 1981).

FEINBERG, J., Social Philosophy (Eaglewood Cliffs: Prentice Hall 1973).

FINIS, J., Natural Law and Natural Rights (Oxford: Clarendon Press,1982).

FISCHER, E., Minorities and Minority Problems (New York: Vantage Press, 1980).

GANJI, M., The Realization of Economic, Social and Cultural Rights Problems, Policies, Progress, (UN S.75 XIV 2 1975).

 - International Protection of Human Rights (1962).

GROS ESPIEL, H., The Right to Self-Determination: Implementation of United Nations Resolutions (UN New York, Doc E/EN 4/SUb.2/405/Rev 1, 1980).

GROMLEY, W.P., Human Rights and Environment; The Need for International Co-operation (Leyden: Sijthoff, 1976).

HARRIS, D.J., Cases and Materials in International Law (London: Sweet & Maxwell, 1991).

HIGGINS, R., The Development of International Law through the Political organ of the United Nations, (London: OUP 1963).

- Human Rights Prospects and Problem (34th Montague Burton Lecture on International Relations)(Leeds: (Leeds Univ. Press 1979).

HONFELD, W.N., Fundamental Legal Conception as applied in Judicial Reasoning (Yale: Yale Univ. Press 1919).

HOBBES, T., Leviathan (1651)(London: Longman 1965).

HUMPHREY, The United Nations charter and UN Declaration of Human Right in Luard (ed.) The International Protection of Human Rights (London: OUP 1967).

JACOBS, F.G., The European Convention on Human Rights (1975) (Oxford: Clarendon Press)

KANYO, (ed.) Human Rights in Africa; Problems and Prospects (NY: International League for Human Rights, 1980).

KAUNDA, D.K., Humanist in Africa (London: OUP 1968).

LAUTERPACHT, H., International Law and Human Rights (1950) (NY: Praeger).

LAQUER, W. & RUBIN, B., (eds.) The Human Rights (NY: New American Library, 1979).

LEVIN, L., Human Rights: Question and Answers (Paris: UNESCO Press, 1975).

MARIE, J.B., La commission des droits de l'homme de l'ONU (Paris: Pedone, 1975).

- Glossary of Human Rights (Paris: Editions de la maison des Sciences de l'homme).

MAZRUI, A., The African Condition (London: Cambridge Univ. Press, 1980).

MCDOUGAL, LASSWELL & LUNG-CHU CHEN, Human Rights and World Public Order, (New Haven: Yale Univ. Press, 1980).

MESTDAGH, K DE V., "The right to development" in Development, Human Right and the Rule of Law(Oxford: Pergamon Press, 1981).

NETTHEIM, G., (ed.) Human Rights for Aboriginal People in the 1980's (Sidney, Aust.: Legal Books 1984).

NOZICK, R., Anarchy, State and Utopia (Oxford:OUP,1974).

NYERERE, J.K., Ujamaa; Essays on Socialism (London: OUP 1968).

OKLIE, C.C., International Law Perspectives of the Developing Countries: The Relationship of Law and Economic Development to basic Human Right (NY:NOH Publishers 1977).

O'MANONY, P.C., The Fantasy of Human Rights, (Essex: Mayhew - Mecrimmon Ltd.,1978)

PELLET, A., Le Droit International de Development (Paris: Presses Universitaires de France,1978).

PORTER, J.N., (ed.) The Right to Life in International Law (Washington, DC: Martinus Nijhoff, The Press of America, 1982).

POMERANCE, M., Self-Determination in Law and Practice. The New Doctrine in the United Nations (The Hague: Martinus Nijhoff, 1982).

RAPHAEL, D.O., Political Theory and the rights of Man (London: Allen & Unwin, 1967).

RASHDOONY, R.Y., Law and liberty (Fairfax: The Burn Press 1977).

RAWLS, J., A Theory of Justice (London: OUP 1972).

ROUSSEAU, J.J., The Social Contract (London: Everyman's Library 1917).

ROBERTSON, A.H., Human Rights in Europe ([2nd ed.] Manchester: Manchester Univ. Press 1977).

- Human Rights in the World, (Manchester 1977).

- (ed.) Human Rights in National and International Law (Manchester: Manch. Univ 1967).

- (ed.) Privacy and Human Rights (Manchester, MUP 1973).

SOHN, L. & BUERGENTHAL, T., The International Protection of Human Rights (1973)(NY: Oceana).

SCHWAB, P., The Response of the left to violence and Human Rights "Abuses" in the Ethiopian Revolution: Towards a Human Rights Framework (NY: Praeger, 1982).

SIEGHART, P., The International Law of Human Rights (Oxford: Clarendon Press, 1983).

TINBERGEN, J., (Co-ordinator) Reshaping the International Order. A Report to the club of Rome(1976 (London: Hutchinson. 1976)

TUCK, R., Natural Rights theories: Their Origin and Development (Cambridge: CUP 1979).

UMOZURIKE, U.O., Self-Determination in International Law (Hamden: Archon Books, 1972).

VAN DYK, P. & VAN HOOF, G.J.H., Theory and Practice of the European Convention on Human Right (Deventer, Netherland: Khiwer law and Taxation Publisher,1984).

VINCENT, R.J., Human Rights and International Relations (Cambridge: CUP 1988).

VAN DER VYVER, J.D., Seven Lectures on Human Rights (Capetown: Juta & Company Ltd., 1978).

VASAK, K., "Human Rights: As a legal reality" in Vasak (ed.) The International Dimension of Human Rights (Westport, CT: Greenwood Press, 1982).

VOGELGEISANG, S., American Dream, Global Nightmares: The dilemma of US Human Rights Policy (NY: Norton 1980).

WALDRON, J., Theories of Rights,(London: OUP), 1984.

A(II): ARTICLES

ABI SAAB, G.M., "Wars of national liberation," Collected Courses, Hague Academy of International Law (1979-IV) Tome 165 (The Hague: Martinus Nijhoff Publish, 1981),p. 353-446.

ALANHANZO, M.G., "Introduction a la charte Africaine des droits de l'homme et des Pueples" in Droit et liberte at la fin du XXe siecle, influence des donnees economiques et technologiques, Editions A. Pedone, Paris, p. 511-37.

ALSTON, P., "Humphrey's Human Rights and the United Nations: A Great Adventure" Book Review in *Human Rights Quarterly* Vol. 6, No. 2, May 1985, p. 224-235.

AMACHREE, G., "Fundamental Rights in Nigeria" *Howard Law Journal* Vol. 11, No. 2, p. 463-500.

AMOAH, P., "The African Charter on Human Rights and People's Rights: Implementation Machinery" Gabrone Conference on Human Rights in Africa 24-29, 1982.

AKPAN, M.E., "The Nigerian Constitution and Human Rights" in Earl M. Coleman(ed.) *Universal Human Rights*, (NY: Stanfordville vol. 2 April - June 1980), p. 23-41.

All African Council of Churches "Factors Responsible for the violations of Human Rights in Africa *Issue*, Vol. 1.

ANIFOWSOE, R., "The Military and Human Rights in Nigeria" Paper presented to the African Association of Political Science, Rabat, 1977.

ASANTE, S.B., "Nation building and Human Rights in emergent African Nations," *Cornell International Law Journal* No. 2, 1969.

BALASURIYA, T., "Organization for Human Rights at the village level" in Human Rights Quarterly No. 3, summer 1981, p. 31-36.

BELLO, E.G., "A Proposal for the Dissemination of International Humanitarian Law in Africa, Pursuant to the 1977 Protocols Additional to the Geneva convention of 1949" *Revue de Droit Penal militaire et le Droit de la Guerre* Societe International de Droit Penale Militaire et de Droit de la Guerre Vol. XXIII, 1-2- 3-4, Bruxelles, 1984, p. 313-323.

- "Shared legal concepts between African customary norms and International Conventions on Humanitarian Law" *Indian Journal of International Law*, Vol. 21, No. 1, Jan - March, 1981, p. 79-95.

BENEDEK, W., "Human Rights in a Multi-cultural Perspective: the African Charter and the Human Rights to Development" in K. Ginther W. Benedek (Hrsg), New Perspectives *and Conceptions of international Law, An Afro-European Dialogue* (Osterreichishe Zeitschrift fur Offenthiches Recht und Volkerrecht, supplement 6), Vienna, p. 147-161.

BERNHARDT, R., "The Protection of fundamental Rights as Community Law is created and Developed: The Problems of drawing up a catalogue of fundamental Rights for the European Communities" *Commission of the European Communities Bulletin* (of the European Communities) Supplement 5/76.

BLACKSTONE W.T., "Equality and Human Rights" *The Monist* 52, 1968.

BOURGET, J.M., (Envoye Special), "Le proces de Bokassa" *VSD* No. 174 31/12/80 - 7/1/81.

BOVEN, Theo, "Human Rights and Responsibilities of the International Civil Services (Studie en Informatiecentrum Menschen-rechten) *Sim Newsletter*, No. 5, Jan. 1984, p. 2-11.

- "The Right to Development and Human Rights," p.49-56 *The Review*, No. 28, June 1982, International Commission Of Jurists, Geneva.

- "The United Nations and Human Rights: Innovation and stagnation," p. 8-20 *Sim Newsletter*, No. 9, Jan 1985.

- "United Nations Policies and Strategies: Global Perspectives" in Ramcharan (ed.) *Human Rights: Thirty Years after the Universal Declaration* (The Hague: Martinus Nijhoff, 1979).

BRANDT, R.B., "The concept of Obligation and Duty," *MIND* Vol. 73, 1964.

CARTER, M., "Human Rights in a One-Party State," *Book Review* International Commission of Jurists (1978).

CARTER, HON R.L., "The Right Not to be separated by Race" *The Supreme Court and Human Rights* (ed.) B. Marshall (Forum series VOA, Washington, 1982).

CASSIN, R., "Quelques souvenir sur la declaration Universelle de 1948 *Revue de Droit contempuraine* 15e annee No. 1/1968.

- La Texte de la Declaration Universelle, *Lumen Vitae*, Vol. XXIII No. 4, Bruxelles, 1968.

CHEN, L.C., "Human rights and the free flow of information" (1982) 4 *NYL Sch. J Int. S Comp .L* 37

CHUNG, S., HAMANYUM, K., & PUNTAMBEKA, S.V., "On the Chinese, Islamic & Hindu Concepts on Human Rights" in the Symposium of UNESCO On Human Rights(1949).

COLIN, J.P. & LANG, J., "La culture entre les peuples et les etats: Vers un nouveau droit International" in Melanges offerts a Charles Chaumont (Paris: A Pedone, 1984),179.

Commission on Human Rights, Reports of the working Group of Governmental Experts on the Rights to Development (E/CN4/1985/11).

DOYLE, M.W., "Kant liberal legacies and foreign affairs" Pf 1 *Philosophy and Public Affairs* Vol. 12 (1983), no. 3.

DUPUY, R.J., "Droit Declaratoire et Droit Programnatoire, de la coutume sauvage a la "soft law" Societe Francaise pour le Droit International; colloque de Toulouse,1974.

ELIAS, T.O., "How the International Court of Justice Deals with request for Advisory opinions" in *Essays in International Law in Honour of Judge Manfred Lachs*,(ed.), Makerezyk Jerzy (The Hague: Martinus Nijhoff Publishers, 1984).

- Methodological problems faced by the I.C.J. in the application of International Law" in Bin Chenji (ed.) *International Law Teaching and Practice* (London: Stevens & Sons, London, 1982).

EMERSON, T.I., "Freedom for Political Speech," in Burke Marshall *The Supreme Court and Human Right* (Washington DC: Forum series/ VOA, 1982), p. 67-74.

EL, AYOUTY, Y., "Thinking about the future of Human Right in Africa" Buffalo Conference on Human Right in Africa 7-9 May 1982.

EZE, O.C., "Rights to Health as a Human Right in Africa" in Rene Jean Dupuy, *Le droit a la sante en tant que de l'homme* (The Hague: Sijhoff and Nordhoff,1979)

FAROUK, A., "Human Life and Development" Some Issues on a low income Country" *Human Rights Quarterly*, Vol. 3, No.3, Summer 1981.

FEGLEY, R., "The United Nations Human Rights Commission: the Equatorial Guinea Case" *Human Rights Quarterly*, Vol. 3, No. 1, Feb. 1981.

FISS, O.W., "Free speech and the prior restraint Doctrine: the Pentagon Papers case" in B. Marshall, The Supreme Court and Human Rights (op. cit.), p. 49-65.

FRIEDMAN, " General Course of Public International Law" *Hague Recueil*, 1969

FROWEIN, J.A., "The European and the American Convention on Human Right - A Comparison" in *Human Right Law Journal* (Keblan Rhein, Strasbourg), Vol. 1, 1980, p. 44-65.

FREDRICH, G., "Rights, liberties freedom: A Reappraisal" *AJI* 57, 1963.

GAINER, G., "Nationalization: the dichotomy between Western and Third World perspectives in International Law" (1983) 26 *Howard L.J.* 1547.

GASTIL, R.D., "Comparative Survey of Freedom" in *Freedom at issue* Jan. - Feb. 1975.

GANSHOF, W.J., "Reliance in the Case law of the European Court of Human Right on the Domestic law of the states" in *Human Rights Law Journal*, Vol. 1, 1980, p. 13-35 (Strasbourg).

GITTLEMAN, R., "The African Commission on Human and People's Rights: Prospects and Procedures" in Hurst Hannum, Guide to International Human Rights Practice(London: Macmillan Press, 1984), p. 153.

GOLDSTEIN, A.S., "Protection Against illegal search and seizure" in B. Marshall, The Supreme Court and Human rights, (op. cit.) p. 179- 85.

HAMALENGWA, M., "The Political Economy of Human Rights in Africa: Historical and Contemporary Perspectus" *Philosophy and Social Action* Vol. 14, No. 3 1983, p. 15-36.

HOWARD, R., "Is there an African Concept of Human Right," working Paper No. A8 Nov. 1983, Development Studies Program, University of Toronto.
- "The full-belly thesis - should Economic Rights take priority over civil and political rights?" Working Paper No. 3 April 1983, Development Studies Program, Univ. of Toronto.
- "Evaluating Human Rights in Africa: some Problems of Implicit comparison" *Human Right Quarterly* Vol. 6, No. 2 May 1984.
- "The Dilemma of Human Right in sub Saharan Africa" *International Journal* Vol. XXXV No. 4, 1980, p. 727-747.

HUDSON " The International Law of the Future, Postulates, Principles and Prospects" 38 *AJIL*, Supp. 41, 1944.

HUMPHREY, "The sub-commission of Discrimination and the Protection of Minorities" *AJIL* Vol. 62, 1968.
- "The Right of Petition in the United Nations" *Human Right Journal* Vol. IV.

KELSEN, "Legal Contribution a l'etude de la revision juridico- technic du statut de la societe des nations", 45 *Revue General de droit international public* (1938)

KHUSHALANI, Y., "Human Rights in Asia and Africa" *Human Right law Journal* 4 (1983), p. 404-442.

KARTCHKIH, Co-operation des pays socialists dans le domaine du droit International *Manuel UNESCO*, Strasbourg, 1976.

KRAMER, D.S., "The 1980 UN Commission on Human Rights and the Disappeared" *Human Right Quarterly* Vol. 3, No. 1, Feb. 1981.

KUNIG, P., "The role of "people's" rights" in the African Charter   on Human and People's Rights in K. Ginther and W. Benedek (ed.) *New perspectives and Conceptions of International Law* (Vienna: Springer Verlag, 1983),p. 147.

LERNER, P., "New Concepts in the UNESCO Declaration on Race and Racial Prejudice," in *Human Right Quarterly* Vol. 3,No. 1, Feb. 1981.

LEJEUNE, A., "Human Rights in African Political Culture" in K.W. Thompson (ed.) *The moral imperatives of Human Rights: A world Survey* (Wash. D.C: U.P.A. 1978).

LEVTZION, N., "Muslim clerics as Defenders of Human Rights in West Africa: Historical Perspectives" Buffalo Conference on Human Rights in Africa, 7-9 May 1982.

M'BAYE, K., "Les realities du Monde Ooir et les droits de l'homme" *Revue des droit de l'homme* (1969).

MARKS, S., "Development and Human Rights; Some reflections on the study of development, Human Right and peace" in *Bulletin of peace Proposals* (1977).

MOWER, A.G., "Human Rights in Black Africa: Double Standard" *Human Rights Journal* No. 10, 1976.

MCDOUGAL, LASSWELL, & CHEN L.C., "Freedom from Discrimination in Choice of Language and International Human Rights" (1976) 50 III *ULJ* 151.

NANDAL, U.P., & others, "Ten years after Stockholm - international environment law" (1984) 79 *Proc ASIL* 411.

 - "Development as an emerging human rights under International Law" (1985) 13 *Denver J Int L 8 Pol* 141.

 - "Economic development and human rights" (1973),67 ASIL, Prog. 198.

NIEC, H., "Human Right to culture" (1979) 44 *Yearbook of the AAA* 109.

OJO, B. A. "La Namibie: Vers l'independance" *Annee Africaine*.1989

OKERE, B.O., "The Protection of Human Right in Africa and the African Charter on Human Rights and People's Rights: A comparative analysis with the European and American systems in *Human Rights Quarterly* Vol. 6,No. 6, May 1984.

OSEIMOKHAI, E.I., "Toward Adequate Defence of Human Rights in Africa" *Indian Journal of International Law* Vol. 21, No. 1, 1981.

OKOLIE, C.C., "Human Rights in Southern Africa, in the Context of Public International Law," *Glendale Law Review*, Vol. 2, 1978.

PAUL, J.C.W., "Law, Socialism and the Human Rights to Development in third world countries" *Review of Socialist Law* Vol. 7, No. 3, 1981, p. 235-242.

PAUL, O., "De la Juridicie des droit economique et sociaux reconnus dans la Declaration Universelle" *Annales des droits, Revue Trimestrielle de droit Belge* XXXIV 1974.

PARTLETT, D., "Benign racial discrimination: equality and Aborigines" (1979) 10 FLR 238.

POLLACK, E.H., (ed.) *Human Rights* (N.Y.: Steward pub. 1971).

ROBERTSON, A.H., "Africa legal Process and the individual" *Revue de droit de l'homme* Vol. 5, 1972.

RAYMOND, J.M., "Genocide: an unconstitutional human rights convention" (1972) 12 Santa *Clara L* 294.

SOHN, L., "UN Machinery for Implementing Human Rights" 62, *AJIL* 1968.

SCHWELB, E., "The International Court of Justice and the Human Rights clauses of the Charter" *AJIL* Vol. 66, 1972.

SZABO, I., "Fondements historiques et development des droits de l'homme, les dimensions internationale du Droit de l'homme *Manuel UNESCO de droit de l'homme* (Provisional edition, Strasbourg).

TCHENCHKO, B., "The concept of human right in the USSR: Comments and Interpretations, *A Symposium, UNESCO* 1949.

ULLMAN, "Human Rights and Economic Process: The US vs. Idi Amin" *Foreign Affairs* Vol. 56, (1978), No. 3.

VELDROSS, A., "La competence nationale dans le cadre de l'organization des nations Unies et l'independence des Etats' *Revue Generale de droit International Public* 1963, No. 2, p. 8-9.

WALDRON, J., "A right to do wrong," *Ethics 92*, 1981.

WEINSTEIN, W., "Human Right in Africa: A long awaited voice," *Current History*, March 1980, Vol. 78, No. 455.

WOOLRIDGE, F. & SHARMA, U.D., "International Law and the expulsion of Uganda Asians," 1975, *J. Int. Law* 30.

ZAKARIYA, H.S., "Sovereignty over natural resources and the search for a New international economic order" in K. Hossain (ed.) *Legal Aspects of the New International Economic Order* (London: Frances Pinter, 1980).

ZAPHIROU, G.A., "Cultural and ideological pluralism and contemporary public International law" (1986) 34 *AJIL* (supp.) 341.

B: SELECTED DOCUMENTS

UNIVERSAL DECLARATION OF HUMAN RIGHTS[1]

PREAMBLE

Whereas recognition of the inherent dignity and of the equal and inalienable rights of all members of the human family is the foundation of freedom, justice and peace in the world.

Whereas disregard and contempt for human rights have resulted in barbarous acts which have outraged the conscience of mankind, and the advent of a world in which human beings shall enjoy freedom of speech and belief and freedom from fear and want has been proclaimed as the highest aspiration of the common people,

Whereas it is essential, if man is not to be compelled to have recourse, as a last resort, to rebellion against tyranny and oppression, that human rights should be protected by the rule of law,

Whereas it is essential to promote the development of friendly relations between nations,

Whereas the peoples of the United Nations have in the Charter reaffirmed their faith in fundamental human rights, in the dignity and worth of the human person and in the equal rights of men and women and have determined to promote social progress and better standards of life in larger freedom,

Whereas Member States have pledged themselves to achieve, in co-operation with the United Nations, the promotion of universal respect for and observance of human rights and fundamental freedoms,

Whereas a common understanding of these rights and freedoms is of the greatest importance for the fall realization of this pledge,

Now, therefore. THE GENERAL ASSEMBLY *proclaims*

This Universal Declaration of Human Rights as a common standard of achievement for all peoples and all nations, to the end that every individual and every organ of society, keeping this Declaration constantly in mind, shall strive by teaching and education to promote respect for these rights and

---

[1] Adopted on 10 December 1948.

freedoms and by progressive measures, national and international, to secure their universal and effective recognition and observance, both among the peoples of Member States themselves and among the peoples of territories under their jurisdiction.

Article 1
All human beings are born free and equal in dignity and rights. They are endowed with reasons and conscience and should act towards one another in a spirit of brotherhood.

Article 2
Everyone is entitled to all the rights and freedoms set forth in this Declaration, without distinction of any kind, such as race, colour, sex, language, religion, political or other opinion, national or social origin, property, birth or other status.
Furthermore, no distinction shall be made on the basis of the political, jurisdictional or international status of the country or territory to which a person belongs, whether it be independent, trust, non-self-governing or under any other limitation of sovereignty.

Article 3
Everyone has the right to life, liberty and the security of person.

Article 4
No one shall be held in slavery or servitude; slavery and slave trade shall be prohibited in all their forms.

Article 5
No one shall be subjected to torture or to cruel, inhuman or degrading treatment or punishment.

Article 6
Everyone has the right to recognition everywhere as a person before the law.

Article 7
All are equal before the law and are entitled without any discrimination to equal protection of the law. All are entitled to equal protection against any

discrimination in violation of this Declaration and against any incitement to such discrimination.

Article 8
Everyone has the right to an effective remedy by the competent national tribunals for acts violating the fundamental rights granted him by the constitution or by law.

Article 9
No one shall be subjected to arbitrary arrest, detention or exile.

Article 10
Everyone is entitled in full equality to a fair and public hearing by an independent and impartial tribunal, in the determination of his rights and obligations and Of any criminal charge against him.

Article 11
1. Everyone charged With a penal offence has the right to be presumed innocent until proved guilty according to law in a public trial at which he has had all the guarantees necessary for his defence.
2. No one shall be held guilty of any penal offence on account of any act or omission which did not constitute a penal offence, under national or international law, at the time when it was committed. Nor shall a heavier penalty be imposed than the one that was applicable at the time the penal offence was committed.

Article 12
No one shall be subjected to arbitrary interference with his privacy, family, home or correspondence, nor to attacks upon his honour and reputation. Everyone has the right to the protection of the law against such interference or attacks.

Article 13
1. Everyone has the right to freedom of movement and residence within the borders Of each State.
2. Everyone his the right to leave any country, including his own, and to return to his country.

Article 14

1. Everyone has the right to seek and to enjoy in other countries asylum from persecution.
2. This right may not be invoked in the case of prosecutions genuinely arising from non-political crimes or from acts contrary to the purposes and principles of the United Nations.

Article 15

1. Everyone has the right to a nationality.
2. No one shall be arbitrarily deprived of his nationality nor denied the right to change his nationality.

Article 16

1. Men and women of full age, without any limitation due to race, nationality Or religion, have the right to marry and to found a family. They are entitled to equal rights as to marriage, during marriage and at its dissolution.
2. Marriage shall be entered into only with the free and full consent of the intending spouses.
3. The family is the natural and fundamental group unit of society and is entitled to protection by society and the State.

Article 17

1. Everyone has the right to own property alone as well as in association with others.
2. No one shall be arbitrarily deprived of his property.

Article 18

Everyone has the right to freedom of thought, conscience and religion; this right includes freedom to change his religion or belief, and freedom, either alone or in community with others and in public or private, to manifest his religion or belief in teaching, practice, worship and observance.

Article 19

Everyone has the right to freedom of opinion and expression; this right includes freedom to hold opinions without interference and to seek, receive and impart information and ideas through any media and regardless of frontiers.

Article 20
1. Everyone has the right to freedom to peaceful assembly and association.
2. No one may be compelled to belong to an association.

Article 21
1 Everyone has the right to take part in the government of his country, directly or through freely chosen representatives.
2. Everyone has the right of equal access to public service in his country.
3. The will of the people shall be the basis of the authority of government; this will shall be expressed in periodic and genuine elections which shall be by universal and equal suffrage and shall be held by secret vote or by equivalent free voting procedures.

Article 22
Everyone, as a member of society, has the right to social security and is entitled to realization, through national effort and international co-operation and in accordance with the organization and resources of each State, of the economic, social and cultural rights indispensable for his dignity and the free development of his personality.

Article 23
1. Everyone has the right to work, to free choice of employment, to just and favourable conditions of work and to protection against unemployment.
2. Everyone, without any discrimination, has the right to equal pay for equal work.
3. Everyone who works has the right to just and favourable remuneration ensuring for himself and his family an existence worthy of human dignity, and supplemented, if necessary, by other means of social protection.
4. Everyone has the right to form and to join trade unions for the protection of his interests.

Article 24
Everyone has the right to rest and leisure, including reasonable limitation of working hours and periodic holidays with pay.

Article 25

1. Everyone has the right to a standard of living adequate for the health and well-being of himself and of his family, including food, clothing, housing and medical care and necessary social services, and the right to security in the event of unemployment, sickness, disability, widowhood, old age or other lack of livelihood in circumstances beyond his control.
2. Motherhood and childhood are entitled to special care and assistance All children, whether born in or out of wedlock, shall enjoy the same social protection.

Article 26

1. Everyone has the right to education. Education shall be free, at least in the elementary and fundamental stages.   Elementary education shall be compulsory.   Technical and professional education shall be made generally available and higher education shall be equally accessible to all on the basis of merit.
2. Education shall be directed to the full development of the human personality and to the strengthening of respect for human rights and fundamental freedoms.   It shall promote understanding, tolerance and friendship among all nations, racial or religious groups, and shall further the activities of the United Nations for the maintenance of peace.
3. Parents have a prior right to choose the kind of education that shall be given to their children.

Article 27

1. Everyone has the right freely to participate in the cultural life of the community, to enjoy the arts and to share in scientific advancement and its benefits.
2. Everyone has the right to the protection of the moral and material interests resulting from any scientific literary or artistic production of which he is the author.

Article 28

Everyone is entitled to a social and international order in which the rights and freedoms set forth in this Declaration can be fully realized.

Article 29

1. Everyone has duties to the community in which alone the free and full development of his personality is possible.
2. In the exercise of his rights and freedoms, everyone shall be subject only to such limitations as are determined by law solely for the purpose of securing due recognition and respect for the rights and freedoms of others and of meeting the just requirements of morality, public order and the general welfare in a democratic society
3. These rights and freedoms May in no case be exercised contrary to the purpose and principles of the United Nations.

Article 30

Nothing in this Declaration maybe interpreted as implying for any State, group or person any right to engage in any activity to perform any act aimed at the destruction of any of the rights and freedoms set forth herein.

INTERNATIONAL COVENANT ON ECONOMIC, SOCIAL AND CULTURAL RIGHTS[1]

PREAMBLE

The States Parties to the Present Covenant,

Considering that, in accordance with the principles proclaimed in the Charter of the United Nations, recognition of the inherent dignity and of the equal and inalienable rights of all members of the human family is the foundation of freedom, justice and peace in the world,

Recognizing that these rights derive from the inherent dignity of the human person,

Recognizing that, in accordance with the Universal Declaration of Human Rights, the ideal of free human beings enjoying freedom from fear and want can only be achieved if conditions are created whereby everyone may enjoy his economic, social and cultural rights, as well as his civil and political rights,

Considering the obligation of States under the Charter of the United Nations to promote universal respect for, and observance of human rights and freedoms,

Realizing that the individual, having duties to other individuals and to the community to which he belongs, is under a responsibility to strive for the promotion and observance of the rights recognized in the present Covenant,

Agree upon the following articles:

PART I

Article 1

1.All peoples have the right of self-determination. By virtue of that right they freely determine their political Status and freely pursue their economic, social and cultural development.

2.All peoples may, for their own ends, freely dispose of their natural wealth and resources without prejudice to any obligations arising out of international economic co-operation, based upon the principle of mutual benefit, and international law. In no case may a people be deprived of its own means of subsistence.

3.The States Parties to the present Covenant, including those having responsibility for the administration of Non-Self-Governing and Trust Territories, shall promote the realization of the right of self-determination, and shall respect that right, in conformity with the provisions of the Charter of the United Nations.

PART II

Article 2

1. Each State Party to the present Covenant undertakes to take steps, individually and through international assistance and co-operation, especially economic and technical, to the maximum of its available resources, with a view to achieving progressively the full realization of the rights recognized in the present Covenant by all appropriate means, including particularly the adoption of legislative measures.

2. The States Parties to the present Covenant undertake to guarantee that the rights enunciated in the present Covenant will be exercised without discrimination of any kind as to race, colour, sex, language, religion, political or other opinion, national or social origin, property, birth or other status.
3. Developing countries, with due regard to human rights and their national economy, may determine to what extent they would guarantee the economic rights recognized in the present Covenant to non-nationals.

Article 3
The States Parties to the present Covenant undertake to ensure the equal right of men and women to the enjoyment of all economic, social and cultural rights set forth in the present Covenant.

Article 4
The States Parties to the present Covenant recognize that, in the enjoyment of those rights provided by the State in conformity with the present Covenant, the State may subject such rights only to such limitations as are determined by law only in so far as this may be compatible with the nature of these rights and solely for the purpose of promoting the general welfare in a democratic Society.

Article 5
1. Nothing in the present Covenant may be interpreted as implying for any State, group or person any right to engage in any activity or to perform any act aimed at the destruction of any of the rights or freedoms recognized herein, or at their limitation to a greater extent than is provided for in the present Covenant.
2. No restriction upon or derogation from any of the fundamental human rights recognized or existing in any country in virtue of law, conventions, regulations or custom shall be admitted on the pretext that the present Covenant does not recognize such rights or that it recognizes them to a lesser extent.

PART III

Article 6

1. The States Parties to the present Covenant recognize the right to work, which includes the right of everyone to the opportunity to gain his living by work which he freely chooses Of accepts, and will take appropriate steps to safeguard this right.

2. The steps to be taken by a State Party to the present Covenant to achieve the full realization of this right shall include technical and vocational guidance and training programmes, policies and techniques to achieve steady economic, social and cultural development and full and productive employment under conditions safeguarding fundamental political and economic freedoms to the individuals

Article 7

The States Parties to the present Covenant recognize the right of everyone to the enjoyment of just and favourable conditions of work which ensure, in particular:

    (a)   Remuneration which provides all workers, as a minimum, with:

    (i) Fair wages and equal remuneration of work of equal value without distinction of any kind, in particular women being guaranteed conditions of work not inferior to those enjoyed by men, with equal pay for equal work;

    (ii) A decent living for themselves and their families in accordance with the provisions of the present Covenant;

    (b)   Safe and healthy working conditions;

    (c)   Equal opportunity for everyone to be promoted in his employment to an   appropriate higher level, subject to no considerations other than those   of seniority and competence;

    (d)   Rest, leisure and reasonable limitation of working hours and periodic holidays with pay, as well as remuneration for public holidays.

Article 8

1. The States Parties to the present Covenant undertake to ensure:

    (a)The right of everyone to form trade unions and join the trade union of his choice, subject only to the rules of the organization concerned, for the promotion and protection of his economic and social interests. No restrictions may be placed on the exercise of this right other than those prescribed by law and which are necessary in a democratic society in the interests of national security or public order or for the protection of the rights and freedoms of others;

(b)The right of trade unions to establish national federations or confederations and the right of the latter to form or join international trade-union organizations;

(c)The right of trade unions to function freely subject to no limitations other than those prescribed by law and which are necessary in a democratic society in the interests of national security or public order or for the protection of the rights and freedoms of others;

(d)The right to strike, provided that it is exercised in conformity with the laws of the particular country.

2. This article shall not prevent the imposition of lawful restrictions on the exercise of these rights by members of the armed forces or of the police or of the administration of the State.

3. Nothing in this article shall authorize States Parties to the International Labour Organisation Convention of 1948 concerning Freedom of Association and Protection of the Right to Organise to take legislative measures which would prejudice, or apply the law in such a manner as would prejudice, the guarantees provided for in that Convention.

Article 9

The States Parties to the present Covenant recognize the right of everyone to social security, including social insurance.

Article 10

The States Parties to the present Covenant recognize that:

1. The widest possible protection and assistance should be accorded to the family, which is the natural and fundamental group unit of society, particularly for its establishment and while it is responsible for the care and education of dependent children. Marriage must be entered into with the free consent of the intending spouses.

2. Special protection should be accorded to mothers during 2 reasonable period before and after childbirth. During such period working mothers should be accorded paid leave or leave with adequate social security benefits.

3. Special measures of protection and assistance should be taken on behalf of all children and young persons without any discrimination for reasons of parentage or other conditions. Children and young persons should be protected from economic and social exploitation. Their employment in work harmful to their morals or health or dangerous to life or likely to hamper their normal development should be punishable by law. States should also set age limits below which the paid employment of child labor should be prohibited and punishable by law.

Article 11
1. The States Parties to the present Covenant recognize the right of everyone to an adequate standard of living for himself and his family, including adequate food, clothing and housing, and to the continuous improvement of living conditions. The States Parties will take appropriate Steps to ensure the realization of this right, recognizing to this effect the essential importance of international co-operation based on free consent.
2. The States Parties to the present Covenant, recognizing the fundamental right of everyone to be free from hunger, shall take, individual and through international co-operation, the measures, including specific programmes, which are needed:
   (a) To improve methods of production, conservation and distribution of food by making full use of technical and scientific knowledge, by disseminating knowledge of the principles of nutrition and by developing or reforming agrarian systems in such 2 way 2S to achieve the most efficient development and utilization of natural resources;
   (b) Taking into account the problems of both food-importing and food-exporting countries, to ensure an equitable distribution of world food supplies in relation to need.

Article 12
1. The States Parties to the present Covenant recognize the right of everyone to the enjoyment of the highest attainable standard of physical and mental health.
2. The steps to be taken by the States Parties to the present Covenant to achieve the full realization of this right shall include those necessary for:
   (a) The provision for the reduction of the still birth-rate and of infant mortality and for the healthy development of the child;

(b)The improvement of all aspects of environmental and industrial hygiene;

(c)The prevention, treatment and control of epidemic, endemic, occupational and other diseases;

(d)The creation of conditions which would assure to all medical service and medical attention in the event of sickness.

Article 13

1. The States Parties to the present Covenant recognize the right of everyone to education. They agree that education shall be directed to the full development of the human personality and the sense of its dignity, and shall strengthen the respect for human rights and fundamental freedoms. They further agree that education shall enable all persons to participate effectively in a free society, promote understanding, tolerance and friendship among all nations and all racial, ethnic or religious groups, and further the activities of the United Nations for the maintenance of Peace.

2. The States Parties to the present Covenant recognize that, with a view to achieving the full realization of this right:

   (a)Primary education shall be compulsory and available free to all;

   (b) Secondary education in its different forms, including technical and vocational secondary education, shall be made generally available and accessible to all by every appropriate means, and in particular by the progressive introduction of free education;

   (c)Higher education shall be made equally accessible to all, on the basis of capacity, by every appropriate means, and in particular by the progressive introduction of free education;

   (d) Fundamental education shall be encouraged or intensified as far as possible for those persons who have not received or completed the whole period of their primary education;

   (e)The development of a system of schools at all levels shall be actively pursued, an adequate fellowship system shall be established, and the material conditions of reaching staff shall be continuously improved.

3. The States Parties to the present Covenant undertake to have the respect for the liberty of parents and, when applicable, legal guardians to choose for their children schools, other than those established by the public authorities, which conform to such minimum educational standards as may be laid down or approved by the State and to ensure the religious and

moral education of their children in conformity with their own convictions.

4. No part of this article shall be construed so as to interfere with the liberty of individuals and bodies to establish and direct educational institutions, subject always to the observance of the principles set forth in paragraph i of this article and to the requirement that the education given in such institutions shall conform to such minimum standards as May be laid down by the State.

Article 14

Each State Party to the present Convention which, at the time of becoming a Party, has not been able to secure in its metropolitan territory or other territories under its jurisdiction compulsory primary education, free of charge, undertakes, within two years, to work out and adopt a detailed plan of action for the progressive implementation, within a reasonable number of years, to be fixed in the plan, of the principle of compulsory education free of charge for all.

Article 15

1. The States Parties to the present Covenant recognize the right of everyone:
   (a) To take part in cultural life;
   (b) To enjoy the benefits of scientific progress- and its applications;
   (c) To benefit from the protection of the moral and material interest: resulting from any scientific, literary or artistic production of which he is the author.
2. The steps to be taken by the States Parties to the present Covenant to achieve the full realization of this right shall include those necessary for the conservation, the development and the diffusion of science and culture.
3. The States Parties to the present Covenant undertake to respect the freedom indispensable for scientific research and creative activity.
4. The States Parties to the present Covenant recognize the benefits to be derived from the encouragement and development of international contacts and cooperation in the scientific and cultural fields.

PART IV

Article 16

1. The States Parties to the present Covenant undertake to submit in conformity with this part of the Covenant reports on the measures which they have adopted and the progress made in achieving the observance of the rights recognized herein.

2. (a) All reports shall be submitted to the Secretary-General of the United Nations, who shall transmit copies to the Economic and Social Council for consideration in accordance with the provisions of the present Covenant;

   (b) The Secretary-General of the United Nations shall also transmit to the specialized agencies copies of the reports, or any relevant parts therefrom, from States Parties to the present Covenant which are also members of these specialized agencies in so far as these reports, or parts therefrom, relate to any matters which fall within the responsibilities of the said agencies in accordance with their constitutional instruments.

Article 17

1. The States Parties to the present Covenant shall furnish their reports in stages, in accordance with a programme to be established by the Economic and Social Council within one year of the entry into force of the present Covenant after consultation with the States Parties and the specialized agencies concerned.

2. Reports may indicate factors and difficulties affecting the degree of fulfillment of obligations under the present Covenant.

3. Where relevant information has previously been furnished to the United Nations or to any specialized agency by any State Party to the present Covenant, it will not be necessary to reproduce that information, but a precise reference to the information so furnished will suffice.

Article 18

Pursuant to its responsibilities under the Charter of the United Nations in the field of human rights and fundamental freedoms, the Economic and Social Council may make arrangements with the specialized agencies in respect of their reporting to it on the progress Made in achieving the observance of the provisions of the present Covenant falling within the scope of their activities.

These reports May include particulars of decisions and recommendations on such implementation adopted by their competent organ.

Article 19

The Economic and Social Council may transmit to the Commission on Human Rights for study and general recommendation or, as appropriate, for information the reports concerning human rights submitted by States in accordance with articles 16 and 17, and those concerning human rights submitted by the specialized agencies in accordance with article 18.

Article 20

The States Parties to the present Covenant and the specialized agencies concerned may submit comments to the Economic and Social Council on any general recommendation under article 19 or reference to such general recommendation in any report of the Commission on Human Rights or any documentation referred to therein.

Article 21

The Economic and Social Council may submit from time to time to the General Assembly reports with recommendations of a general nature and a summary of the information received from the States Parties to the present Covenant and the Specialized agencies on the measures taken and the progress made in achieving general observance of the rights recognized in the present Covenant.

Article 22

The Economic and Social Council may bring to the attention of other organs of the United Nations, their subsidiary organs and specialized agencies concerned with furnishing technical assistance any matters arising out of the reports referred to in this part of the present Covenant which may assist such bodies in deciding, each within its field of competence, on the advisability of international measures likely to contribute to the effective progressive implementation of the present Covenant.

Article 23

The States Parties to the present Covenant agree that international action for the achievement of the rights recognized in the present Covenant includes such methods as the conventions, the adoption of recommendations, the furnishing of technical assistance and the holding of regional meetings and technical meetings for the purpose of consultation and study organized in conjunction with the Governments concerned.

Article 24
Nothing in the present Covenant shall be interpreted as impairing the provisions of the Charter of the United Nations and of the constitutions of the specialized agencies which define the respective responsibilities of tile various organs of the United Nations and of the specialized agencies in regard to the matters dealt with in the present Covenant.

Article 25
Nothing in the present Covenant shall be interpreted as impairing the inherent right of all peoples to enjoy and utilize fully and freely their natural wealth and resources.

PART V

Article 26
1. The present Covenant is open for signature by any State Member of the United Nations or member Of any of its specialized agencies, by any State Party to the Statute of the International Court of justice, and by any other State which has been invited by the General Assembly of the United Nations to become a party to the present Covenant.
2. The present Covenant is subject to ratification. Instruments of ratification shall be deposited with the Secretary-General of the United Nations.
3. The present Covenant shall be open to accession by any State referred to in paragraph I of this article.
4. Accession shall be effected by the deposit Of an instrument of accession with the Secretary-General of the United Nations.
5. The Secretary-General of the United Nations shall inform all States which have signed the present Covenant or acceded to it of the deposit of each instrument of ratification or accession.

Article 27

1. The present Covenant shall enter into force three months after the date of the deposit with the Secretary-General of the United Nations of the thirty-fifth instrument of ratification or instrument Of accession.
2. For each State ratifying the present Covenant or acceding to it after the deposit of the thirty-fifth instrument Of ratification or instrument of accession, the present Covenant shall enter into force three months after the date of the deposit of its own instrument of ratification or instrument of accession.

Article 28

The provisions of the present Covenant shall extend to all parts of federal States without any limitations or exceptions.

Article 29

1. Any State Party to the present Covenant may propose an amendment and file it with the Secretary-General of the United Nations. The Secretary General shall thereupon communicate any proposed amendments to the States Parties to the present Covenant with a request that they notify him whether they favour a conference of States Parties for the purpose of considering and voting upon the proposals. In the event that at least one third of the States Parties favours such a conference, the Secretary-General shall convene the conference under the auspices of the United Nations. Any amendment adopted by a majority of the States Parties present and voting at the conference shall be submitted to the General Assembly of the United Nations for approval.
2. Amendments shall come into force when they have been approved by the General Assembly of the United Nations and accepted by a two-thirds majority of the States Parties to the present Covenant in accordance with their respective constitutional processes.
3. When amendments come into force they shall be binding on those States Parties which have accepted them, other States Parties still being bound by the provisions of the present Covenant and any earlier amendment which they have accepted.

Article 30

Irrespective of the notifications made under article 26, paragraph 5, the Secretary-General of the United Nations shall inform all States referred to in paragraph I of the same article of the following particulars:

    (a) Signatures, ratifications and accessions under article 26;

    (b) The date of the entry into force of the present Covenant under article 27 and the date of the entry into force of any amendments under article 29.

Article 31

1. The present Covenant, of which the Chinese, English, French, Russian and Spanish texts are equally authentic, shall be deposited in the archives of the United Nations.

2. The Secretary-General of the United Nations shall transmit certified copies of the present Covenant to all States referred to in article 26.

INTERNATIONAL COVENANT ON CIVIL AND POLITICAL RIGHTS[2]

PREAMBLE

The States Parties to the Present Covenant,

    Considering that, in accordance with the principles proclaimed in the Charter of the United Nations, recognition of the inherent dignity and of the equal and inalienable rights of all members of the human family is the foundation of freedom, justice and peace in the world,

    Recognizing that these rights derive from the inherent dignity of the human person,

    Recognizing that, in accordance with the Universal Declaration of Human Rights, the ideal of free human beings enjoying civil and political freedom and freedom from fear and want can only be achieved if conditions are created whereby everyone may enjoy his civil and political rights, as well as his economic, social and cultural rights,

---

[2] In force since March 23, 1976

Considering the obligation of States under the Charter of the United Nations to promote universal respect for, and observance of, human rights and freedoms,

Realizing that the individual, having duties to other individuals and to the community to which lie belongs, is under a responsibility to strive for the promotion and observance of the rights recognized in the present Covenant,

Agree upon the following articles:

PART 1

Article 1

1. All peoples have the right or self-determination. By virtue of that right they freely determine their political status and freely pursue their economic, social and cultural development.

2. All peoples may, for their own ends, freely dispose of their natural wealth and resources without prejudice to any obligations arising out of international economic cooperation, based upon the principle of mutual benefits and international law, In no case may a people be deprived of its own means of subsistence.

3. The States Parties to the present Covenant, including those having responsibility for the administration of Non-Self-Governing and Trust Territories, shall promote the realization of the right of self-determination, and shall respect that right, in conformity with the provisions of the Charter of the United Nations.

PART II

Article 2

1. Each State Party to the present Covenant undertakes to respect and to ensure to all individuals within its territory and subject to its jurisdiction the rights recognized in the present Covenant, without distinction Of any kind, Such as race, colour, sex, language, religion, political or other opinion, national or social origin, property, birth or other status.

2. Where not already provided for by existing legislative or other measures, each State Party to the present Covenant undertakes to take the necessary

steps, in accordance with its constitutional processes and with the provisions of the present Covenant, to adopt such legislative or other measures as may be necessary to give effect to the rights recognized in the present Covenant.

3. Each State Party to the present Covenant undertakes:

    (a) To ensure that any person whose rights or freedoms as herein recognized are violated shall have an effective remedy, notwithstanding that the violation has been committed by persons acting in an official capacity;

    (b) To ensure that any person claiming such a remedy shall have his right thereto determined by competent judicial, administrative or legislative authorities, or by any other competent authority provided for by the legal system of the State, and to develop the possibilities of judicial remedy;

    (c) To ensure that the competent authorities shall enforce such remedies when granted.

Article 3

The States Parties to the present Covenant undertake to ensure the equal right of men and women to the enjoyment of all civil and political rights set forth in the present Covenant.

Article 4

1. In time of public emergency which threatens the life of the nation and the existence of which is officially proclaimed, the States Parties to the present Covenant may take measures derogating from their obligations under the present Covenant to the extent strictly required by the exigencies of the situation, provided that such measures are not inconsistent with their other obligations under international law and do not involve discrimination solely on the ground of race, colour, sex, language, religion or social origin.

2. No derogation from articles 6, 7, 8 (paragraphs I and 2),11, 15,16 and 18 may be made under this provision.

3. Any State Party to the present Covenant availing itself of the right of derogation shall immediately inform the other States Parties to the present Covenant, through the intermediary of the Secretary-General of the United Nations, of the provisions from which it has derogated and of the reasons

by which it was actuated. A further communication shall be made, through the same intermediary, on the date on which it terminates such derogation.

Article 5

1. Nothing in the present Covenant may be interpreted as implying for any State, group or person any right to engage in any activity or perform any act aimed at the destruction of any of the rights and freedoms recognized herein or at their limitation to a greater extent than is provided for in the present Covenant.
2. There shall be no restriction upon or derogation from any of the fundamental human rights recognized or existing in any State Party to the present Covenant pursuant to law, conventions, regulations or custom on the pretext that the present Covenant does not recognize such rights or that it recognizes them to a lesser extent.

PART III

Article 6

1. Every human being has the inherent right to life. This right shall be protected by law. No one shall be arbitrarily deprived of his life.
2. In countries which have not abolished the death penalty, sentence of death may be imposed only for the most serious crimes in accordance with the law in force at the time of the commission of the crime and not contrary to the provisions of the present Covenant and to the Convention on tile Prevention and Punishment of the Crime of Genocide. This penalty can only be carried out pursuant to a final judgement tendered by a competent court.
3. When deprivation of life constitutes the crime of genocide, it is understood that nothing in this article shall authorize any State Party to the present Covenant to derogate in any way from any obligation assumed under the provisions of the Convention on the Prevention and Punishment of the Crime of Genocide.
4. Anyone sentenced to death shall have the right to seek pardon or commutation of the sentence. Amnesty, pardon or commutation of the sentence of death may be granted in all cases.

5. Sentence of death shall not he imposed for crimes committed by persons below eighteen years of age and shall not be carried out on pregnant women.
6. Nothing in this article shall be invoked to delay or to prevent the abolition of capital punishment by any State party to the present Covenant.

Article 7
No one shall be subjected to torture or to cruel, inhuman or degrading treatment or punishment. In particular, no one shall be subjected without his free consent to medical or scientific experimentation.

Article 8
1. No one shall be field in slavery; slavery and the slave-trade in all their forms shall be prohibited.
2. No one shall be held in servitude.
3. (a) No one shall be required to perform forced or compulsory labour,
   (b) Paragraph 3 (a) shall not be held to preclude, in countries where imprisonment with hard labour may be imposed as a punishment for a crime, the performance of hard labour in pursuance of a sentence to such punishment by a competent court:
   (c) For the purpose of this paragraph the term "forced or compulsory labour" shall not include:
      (i) Any work or service, not referred to in subparagraph (b), normally required of a person who is under detention in consequence of a lawful order of a court, or of a person during conditional release from such detention;
      (ii) Any service of a military character and, in countries where conscientious objection is recognized, any national service required by law of conscientious objectors;
      (iii) Any service exacted in cases of emergency or calamity threatening the life or well-being of the community;
      (iv) Any work or service which forms part of normal civil obligations.

Article 9
1. Everyone has the right to liberty and security of person. No one shall be subjected to arbitrary arrest or detention. No one shall be deprived of his

liberty except on such grounds and in accordance with such procedure as are established by law.

2. Anyone who is arrested shall be informed, at the time Of arrest, of the reasons for his arrest and shall be promptly informed Of any charges against him.

3. Anyone arrested or detained on a criminal charge shall be brought promptly before a judge or other officer authorized by law to exercise judicial power and shall be entitled to trial within a reasonable time or to release. It shall not be the general rule that persons awaiting trial shall be detained in custody, but release may be subject to guarantees to appear for trial at any other stage of the judicial proceedings, and should occasion arise, for execution of judgment.

4. Anyone who is deprived of his liberty by arrest or detention shall be entitled to take proceedings before a court, in order that that court may decide without delay on the lawfulness of his detention and order his release if the detention is not lawful.

5. Anyone who has been the victim of unlawful arrest or detention shall have an enforceable right to compensation.

Article 10

1. All person, deprived of their liberty shall be treated with humanity and with respect for the inherent dignity of the human person.

2. (a)Accused persons shall, save in exceptional circumstances, be segregated from convicted persons and shall be subject to separate treatment appropriate to their status as unconvicted persons;
   (b)Accused juvenile persons shall be separated from adults and brought as speedily as possible for adjudication.

3. The penitentiary system shall comprise treatment of prisoners the essential aim of which shall be their reformation and social rehabilitation. Juvenile offenders shall be segregated from the adults and be accorded treatment appropriate to their age and legal status.

Article 11

No one shall be imprisoned merely on the ground of inability to fulfil a contractual obligation.

Article 12

1. Everyone lawfully within the territory of a State shall, within that territory, have the right to liberty of movement and freedom to choose his residence.
2. Everyone shall be free to leave any country, including his own.
3. The above-mentioned rights shall not be subject to any restrictions except those which arc provided by law, are necessary to protect national security, public order (order public), public health or morals or the rights and freedoms of others, and are consistent with the other rights recognized in the present Covenant.
4. No one shall be arbitrarily deprived of the right to enter his own country.

Article 13

An alien lawfully in the territory of a State Party to the present Covenant may be expelled therefrom only in pursuance of a decision reached in accordance with law and shall, except where compelling reasons of national security otherwise require, he allowed to submit the reason against his expulsion and to have his case reviewed by, and be presented for the purpose before, the competent authority or a person or persons especially designated by the competent authority.

Article 14

1. All persons shall be equal before the courts and tribunals. In the determination of any criminal charge against him, or of his rights and obligations in a suit at law, everyone shall he entitled to a fair and public hearing by a competent, independent and impartial tribunal established by law. The Press and the public may be excluded from all or part of a trial for reasons of morals, public order (order public) or national security in a democratic society, or when the interest of the private lives of the parties so requires, or to the extent strictly necessary in the opinion of the court in special circumstances where publicity would prejudice the interests of justice; but any judgement rendered in a criminal case or in a suit at law shall be made public except where the interest of juvenile persons otherwise requires or the proceedings concern matrimonial disputes or the guardianship of children.
2. Everyone charged with a criminal offence shall have the right to be presumed innocent until proved guilty according to law.

3. In the determination Of any criminal charge against him, everyone entitled to the following minimum guarantees, in full equality:

    (a) To be informed promptly and in detail in a language which he understands of the nature and cause of the charge against him;

    (b) To have adequate time and facilities for the preparation of his defence and to communicate with counsel of his own choosing;

    (c) To be tried without undue delay;

    (d) To be tried in his presence, and to defend himself in person or through legal assistance of his own choosing; to be informed, if he does not have legal assistance, of this right; and to have legal assistance assigned to him, in any case where the interests of justice so require, and without payment by him in any such case if he does not have sufficient means to pay for it;

    (e) To examine, or have examined, the witnesses against him and to obtain the attendance and examination of witnesses on his behalf under the same conditions as witnesses against him;

    (f) To have the free assistance of an interpreter if he cannot understand or speak the language used in court;

    (g) Not to be compelled to testify against himself or to confess guilt.

4. In the case of juvenile persons, the procedure shall be such as will take account of their age and the desirability of promoting the rehabilitation.

5   Everyone convicted of a crime shall have the right to his conviction and sentence being reviewed by a higher tribunal according to law.

6. When a person has by a final decision been convicted of a criminal offence and when subsequently his conviction has been reversed or he has been pardoned on the ground that a new or newly discovered fact shows conclusively that there has been a miscarriage of justice, the person who has suffered punishment as a result of such conviction shall be compensated according to law, unless it is proved that the non-disclosure of the unknown fact in time is wholly or partly attributable to him.

7. No one shall be liable to be tried or punished again for an offence for which he has already been finally convicted or acquitted in accordance with the law and penal procedure of each country.

Article 15

1. No one shall be held guilty of any criminal offence on account of any act or omission which did not constitute a criminal offence, under national or

international law, at the time when it was committed. Nor shall a heavier penalty be imposed than the one that was applicable at the time when the criminal offence was committed. If, subsequent to the commission of the offence, provision is made by law for the imposition of a lighter penalty, the offender shall benefit thereby.

2. Nothing in this article shall prejudice the trial and punishment of any person for any act or omission which, at the time when it was committed, was criminal according to the general principles of law recognized by the community of nations.

Article 16

Everyone shall have the right to recognition everywhere as a person before the law.

Article 17

1. No one shall be subjected to arbitrary or unlawful interference with his privacy, family, home or correspondence, nor to unlawful attacks on his honour and reputation.
2. Everyone has the right to the protection of the law against such interference or attacks.

Article 18

1. Everyone shall have the right to freedom of thought, conscience and religion. This right shall include freedom to have or to adopt a religion or belief of his choice, and freedom, either individually or in community with others and in public or private, to manifest his religion or belief in worship, observance, practice and teaching.
2. No one shall be subject to coercion which would impair his freedom to have or to adopt to religion or belief of his choice.
3. Freedom to manifest one's religion or beliefs may be subject only to such limitations as are prescribed by law and are necessary to protect public safety, order, health, or morals or the fundamental rights and freedoms of others.
4. The States Parties to the present Covenant undertake to have respect for the liberty of parents and, when applicable, legal guardians to ensure the religious and moral education of their children in conformity with their own convictions.

Article 19

1. Everyone shall have the right to hold opinions without interference.
2. Everyone shall have the right to freedom of expression; this right shall include freedom to seek, receive and impart information and ideas of all kinds. regardless of frontiers, either orally, in writing or in print, in the form of art, or through any other media of his choice.
3. The exercise of the rights provided for in paragraph 2 of this article carries with it special duties and responsibilities. It may therefore be subject to certain restrictions, but these shall only be such as are provided by law and are necessary

    (a)For respect of the rights or reputations of others;

    (b)For the protection of national security or of public order (*ordre public*) or of public health or morals.

Article 20

1. Any propaganda for war shall be prohibited by law.
2. Any advocacy of national, racial or religious hatred that constitutes incitement to discrimination, hostility or violence shall be prohibited by law.

Article 21

The right of peaceful assembly shall be recognized. No restrictions may be placed on the exercise of this right other than those imposed in conformity with the law and which are necessary in a democratic society in the interests of national security or public safety, public order (*ordre public*), the protection of public health or morals or the protection of the rights and freedoms of others.

Article 22

1. Everyone shall have the right to freedom of association with others including the right to form and join trade unions for the protection of his interests.
2. No restrictions may be placed on the exercise of this right other than those which are prescribed by law and which are necessary in a democratic society in the interests of national security or public safety, public order (*ordre public*), the protection of public health or morals or the protection of the rights and freedoms of others. This article shall not prevent the

imposition of lawful restrictions on members of the armed forces and of the police in their exercise of this right.

3. Nothing in this article shall authorize States Parties to the International Labour Organisation Convention of 1948 concerning Freedom of Association and Protection of the Right to Organise to take legislative measures which would prejudice, or to apply the law in such a manner as to prejudice, the guarantees provided for in that Convention.

Article 23

1. The family is the natural and fundamental group unit of society and is entitled to protection by society and the State.
2. The right of men and women of marriageable age to marry and to found a family shall be recognized.
3. No marriage shall be entered into without the free and full consent of the intending spouses.
4. States Parties to the present Covenant shall take appropriate steps to ensure equality of rights and responsibilities of spouses as to marriage, during marriage and at its dissolution. In the case of dissolution, provision shall be made for the necessary protection of any children.

Article 24

1. Every child shall have, without any discrimination as to race, colour, sex, language, religion, national or social origin, property or birth, the right to such measures of protection as are required by his status as a minor, on the part of his family, society and the State.
2. Every child shall be registered immediately after birth and shall have a name.
3. Every child has the right to acquire a nationality.

Article 25

Every citizen shall have the right and the opportunity, without any of the distinctions mentioned in article 2 and without unreasonable restrictions:

   (a).To take part in the conduct of public affairs, directly or through freely chosen representatives;
   (b).To vote and to be elected at genuine periodic elections which shall be by universal and equal suffrage and shall be held by secret ballot, guaranteeing the free expression of the will of the electors;

(c).To have access, on general terms of equality, to public service in his country.

Article 26

All persons, are equal before the law and are entitled without any discrimination to the equal protection of the law. In this respect, the law shall prohibit any discrimination and guarantee to 211 persons equal 1 and effective protection against discrimination on any ground such as race, colour, sex, language, religion, political or other opinion, national or social origin, property, birth or other Status.

Article 27

In those States in which ethnic, religious or linguistic minorities exist, persons belonging to such minorities shall not be denied the right, in community with the other members of their group, to enjoy their own culture, to profess and practice their own religion, or to use their own language.

PART IV

Article 28

1. There shall be established a Human Rights Committee (hereafter referred to in the present Covenant as the Committee). It shall consist of eighteen members and shall carry out the functions hereinafter provided.
2. The Committee shall be composed of nationals of the States Parties to the present Covenant who shall be persons of high moral character and recognized competence in the field of human rights, consideration being given to the usefulness of the participation of some persons having legal experience.
3. The members of the Committee shall be elected and shall sme in their personal capacity.

Article 29

1. The members of the Committee shall be elected by secret ballot from a list of persons possessing the qualifications prescribed in article 28 and nominated for the purpose by the States Parties to the present Covenant.
2. Each State Party to the present Covenant may nominate not more than two persons. These persons shall be nationals of the nominating State.
3. A person shall be eligible for re-nomination.

Article 30

1. The initial election shall be held no later than six months after the date of the entry into force of the present Covenant.

2. At least four months before the date of each election to the Committee, other than an election to fill a vacancy declared in accordance with article 34, the Secretary-General of the United Nations shall address a written invitation to the States Parties to the present Covenant to submit their nominations for membership of the Committee within three months.

3. The Secretary-General of the United Nations shall prepare a list in alphabetical order of all the persons thus nominated, with an indication of the States Parties which have nominated them, and shall submit it to the States Parties to the present Covenant no later than one month before the date Of each election.

4. Elections of the members of the Committee shall be held at a meeting of the States Parties to the present Covenant convened by the Secretary-General of the United Nations at the Headquarters of the United Nations. At that meeting, for which two thirds of the States Parties to the present Covenant shall constitute a quorum, the persons elected to the Committee shall be those nominees who obtain the largest number of votes and an absolute majority of the votes of the representatives of States Parties present and voting.

Article 31

1. The Committee may not include more than one national of the same State.

2. In the election of the Committee, consideration shall be given to equitable geographical distribution of membership and to the representation of the different forms of civilization and of the principal legal systems.

Article 32

1. The members of the Committee shall be elected for a term of four years. They shall be eligible for re-election if renominated, However, the terms of nine of the members elected at the first election shall expire at the end of two years; immediately after the first election, the names of these nine members shall be chosen by lot by the Chairman of the meeting referred to in article 30, paragraph 4.

2.Elections at the expiry of office shall be held in accordance with the preceding articles of this part of the present Covenant.

Article 33

1.If, in the unanimous opinion of the other members, a member of the Committee has ceased to carry out his functions for any cause other than absence of a temporary character, the Chairman of the Committee shall notify the Secretary-General of the United Nations, who shall then declare the seat of that member to be vacant.

2.In the event of the death or the resignation of a member of the Committee, the Chairman shall immediately notify the Secretary-General of the United Nations, who shall declare the seat vacant from the date of death or the date on which the resignation takes effect.

Article 34

1. When a vacancy is declared in accordance with article 33 and if the term of office of the member to be replaced does not expire within six months of the declaration of the vacancy, the Secretary-General of the United Nations, who shall notify each of the States Parties to the present Covenant, which may within two months submit nominations in accordance with article 29for the purpose of filling the vacancy.

2. The Secretary-General of the United Nations shall prepare a list in alphabetical order of the persons thus nominated and shall submit it to the States Parties to the present Covenant. The election to fill the vacancy shall then take place in accordance with the relevant provisions of this part of the present Covenant.

3. A member of the Committee elected to fill a vacancy declared in accordance with article 33 shall hold office for the remainder of the term of the member who vacated the seat on the Committee under the provisions of that article.

Article 35

The members of the Committee shall, with the approval of the General Assembly of the United Nations, receive emoluments from United Nations resources on such terms and conditions as the General Assembly may decide, having regard to the importance of the Committee's responsibilities.

Article 36

The Secretary-General of the United Nations shall provide the necessary staff and facilities for the effective performance of the functions of the Committee under the present Covenant.

Article 37

1. The secretary General of the United Nations shall convene the initial meeting of the Committee at the Headquarters of the United Nations.
2. After its initial meeting, the Committee shall meet at such times as shall be provided in its rules of procedure.
3. The Committee shall normally meet at the Headquarters of the United Nations or at the United Nations Office at Geneva.

Article 38

Every member of the Committee shall, before taking up his duties, make a solemn declaration in open committee that he will perform his functions impartially and conscientiously.

Article 39

1. The Committee shall elect its Officers for I term of two years. They may be re-elected.
2. The Committee shall establish its own rules of procedure, but these rules shall provide, inter alia, that:
   (a)Twelve members shall constitute a quorum;
   (b)Decisions of the Committee shall be made by a majority vote of the members present.

Article 40

1. The States Parties to the present Covenant undertake to submit reports on the measures they have adopted which give effect to the rights recognized herein and on the progress made in the enjoyment of those rights:
   (a)Within one year of the entry into force of the present Covenant for the States Parties concerned;
   (b) Thereafter whenever the Committee so requests.
2. All reports shall be submitted to the Secretary-General of the United Nations, who shall transmit them to the Committee for consideration.

Reports shall indicate the factors and difficulties, if any, affecting the implementation of the present Covenant.

3. The Secretary-General of the United Nations may, after consultation with the Committee, transmit to the specialized agencies concerned copies of such parts of the reports as may fall within their field of competence.

4. The Committee shall study the reports submitted by the States Parties to the present Covenant. It shall transmit its reports, and such general comments as it may consider appropriate, to the States Parties. The Committee may also transmit to the Economic and Social Council these comments along with the copies of the reports it has received from States Parties to the present Covenant.

5. The States Parties to the present Covenant may submit to the Committee observations on any comments that may be made in accordance with paragraph 4 of this article.

Article 41

1. A State Party to the present Covenant may at any time declare under this article that it recognizes the competence of the Committee to receive and consider communications to the effect that a State Party claims that another State Parry is not fulfilling its obligations under the present Covenant. Communications under this article may be received and considered only if submitted by a State Party which has made a declaration recognizing in regard to itself the competence of the Committee. No communication shall be received by the Committee if it concerns a State Party which has not made such a declaration. Communications received under this article shall be dealt with in accordance with the following procedure:

   (a)If a State Party to the present Covenant considers that another State Party is not giving effect to the provisions of the present Covenant, it may, by written communication, bring the matter to the attention of that State Party. Within three months after the receipt of the communication, the receiving State shall afford the State which sent the communication an explanation or any other statement in writing clarifying the matter, which should include, to the extent possible and pertinent, reference to domestic procedures and remedies taken, pending, or available in the matter.

(b) If the matter is not adjusted to the satisfaction of both States Parties concerned within six months after the receipt by the receiving State of the initial communication, either State shall have the right to refer the matter to the Committee, by notice given to the Committee and to the other State.

(c) The Committee shall deal with a matter referred to it only after it has ascertained that all available domestic remedies have been invoked and exhausted in the matter, in conformity with the generally recognized principles of international law. This shall not be the rule where the application of the remedies is unreasonably prolonged.

(d) The Committee shall hold closed meetings when examining communications under this article.

(e) Subject to the provisions of subparagraph (c), the Committee shall make available its good offices to the States Parties concerned with a view to a friendly solution of the matter on the basis of respect for human rights and fundamental freedoms as recognized in the present Covenant.

(f) In any matter referred to it, the Committee may call upon the States Parties concerned, referred to in subparagraph (b), to supply any relevant information.

(g) The States Parties concerned, referred to in subparagraph (b), shall have the right to be represented when the matter is being considered in the Committee and to make submissions orally and/or in writing.

(h) The Committee shall, within twelve months after the date of receipt of notice under subparagraph (b), submit a report:

(i) If a solution within the terms of subparagraph (e) is reached, the Committee shall confine its report to 2 brief statement of the facts and of the solution reached;

(ii) If a solution within the terms of subparagraph (e) is not reached, the Committee shall confine its report to a brief statement of the facts; the written submissions and record of the oral submissions made by the States Parties concerned shall attached to the report. In every matter, the report shall be communicated to the States Parties concerned.

2. The provisions of this article shall come into force when the States Parties to the present Covenant have made declarations under paragraph I of this article. Such declarations shall be deposited by the States Parties with the

Secretary-General of the United Nations, who shall transmit copies thereof to the other States Parties. A declaration may be withdrawn at any time by notification to the Secretary-General. Such a withdrawal shall not prejudice the consideration of any matter which is the subject of a communication already transmitted under this article; no further communication by any State Party shall be received after the notification of withdrawal of the declaration has been received by the Secretary-General, unless the State Party concerned has made new declaration.

OPTIONAL PROTOCOL TO THE INTERNATIONAL COVENANT ON CIVIL AND POLITICAL RIGHTS[3]

The States Parties to the Present Protocol,
Considering that in order further to achieve the purposes of the Covenant on Civil and Political Rights (hereinafter referred to as the Covenant) and the implementation of its provisions it would be appropriate to enable the Human Rights Committee set up in part IV of the Covenant (hereinafter referred to as the Committee) to receive and consider, as provided in the present Protocol, communications from individuals claiming to be victims of violations of any of the rights set forth in the Covenant,
Have agreed as follows:

Article 1
A State Party to the Covenant that becomes a party to the present Protocol recognizes the competence of the Committee to receive and consider communications from individuals subject to its jurisdiction who claim to be victims of a violation by that State Party of any of the rights set forth in the Covenant. No communication shall be received by the Committee if it concerns a State Party to the Covenant which is not a party to the present Protocol.
Article 2
Subject to the provisions of article 1, individuals who claim that any of their rights enumerated in the Covenant have been violated and who have

---

[3] In Force since March 23, 1976

exhausted all available domestic remedies may submit a written communication to the Committee for consideration.

Article 3
The Committee shall consider inadmissible any communication under the present Protocol which is anonymous, or which it considers to be an abuse of the right of submission of such communications or to be incompatible with the provisions of the Covenant.

Article 4
1. Subject to the provisions of article 3, the Committee shall bring, any communications submitted to it under the present Protocol to the attention of the State Party to the present Protocol alleged to be violating any provision of the Covenant.
2. Within six months, the receiving State shall submit to the Committee written explanations or statements clarifying the matter and the remedy if any, that may have been taken by that State.

Article 5
1. The Committee shall consider communications received under the present Protocol in the light of all written information made available to it by the individual and by the State Party concerned.
2. The Committee shall not consider any communication from an individual unless it has ascertained that:
   (a)The same matter is not being examined-under another procedure of international investigation of settlement;
   (b)The individual has exhausted all available domestic remedies. This shall nor be the rule where the application of the remedies is unreasonably prolonged.
3. The Committee shall hold closed meetings when examining communications under the present Protocol.
4. The Committee shall forward its views to the State Party concerned and to the individual.

Article 6
The Committee shall include in its annual report under article 45 of the Covenant a summary of its activities under the present Protocol.

Article 7

Pending the achievement of the objectives of resolution 1514 (XV) adopted by the General Assembly of the United Nations on 14 December 1960 concerning the Declaration on the Granting of Independence to Colonial Countries and Peoples, the provisions of the present Protocol shall in no Way limit the right of petition granted to these peoples by the Charter of the United Nations and other international conventions and instruments under the United Nations and its specialized agencies.

Article 8

1. The present Protocol is open for signature by any State which has signed the Covenant.
2. The present Protocol is subject to ratification by any State which has ratified or acceded to the Covenant. Instruments of ratification shall be deposited with the Secretary-general of the United Nations.
3. The present Protocol shall be open to accession by any State which has ratified or acceded to the Covenant.
4. Accession shall be effected by the deposit of an instrument of accession with the Secretary-General of the United Nations.
5. The Secretary-General of the United Nations shall inform 211 States which have signed the present Protocol or acceded to it of the deposit of each instrument Of ratification or accession.

Article 9

1. Subject to the entry into force of the Covenant, the present Protocol shall enter into force three months after the date of the deposit with the Secretary-General Of the United Nations of the tenth instrument of ratification or instrument of accession.
2. For each State ratifying the present Protocol or acceding to it after the deposit of the tenth instrument of ratification or instrument of accession, the present Protocol shall enter into force three months after the date of the deposit of its own instrument of ratification or instrument Of accession.

Article 10

The provisions of the present Protocol shall extend to all parts of federal States without any limitations or exceptions.

Article 11

1. Any State Party to the present Protocol may propose an amendment and file it with the Secretary-General of the United Nations. The Secretary - General shall thereupon communicate any proposed amendments to the States Parties to the present Protocol with a request that they notify him whether they favour a conference Of States Parties for the purpose of con- sidering and voting upon the proposal. In the event that at least one third of the States Parties favours such a conference, the Secretary-General shall convene the conference under the auspices of the United Nations. Any amendment adopted by a majority of the States Parties present and voting at the conference shall be submitted to the General Assembly of the United Nations for approval.

2. Amendments shall come into force when they have been approved by the General Assembly of the United Nations and accepted by a two-thirds majority of the States Parties to the present Protocol in accordance with their respective constitutional processes.

3. When amendments come into force, they shall be binding on those States Parties which have accepted them, other States Parties still being bound by the provisions of the present Protocol and any earlier amendment which they have accepted.

Article 12

1. Any State Party may denounce the present Protocol at any time by written notification addressed to tile Secretary-General of the United Nations. Denunciation shall take effect three months after the date of receipt of the notification by the Secretary-General.

2. Denunciation shall be without prejudice to the continued application of tile provisions of the present Protocol to any communication submitted under article 2 before the effective date of denunciation.

Article 13

Irrespective of the notifications made under article 8, paragraph 5, of the present Protocol, the Secretary-General of the United Nations shall inform all States referred to in article 48, paragraph 1, of the Covenant of the following particulars:

(a) Signatures, ratifications and accessions under article 8;

(b) The date of the entry into force of the present Protocol under article 9

and the date of the entry into force of any amendments under article 11;
(c) Denunciations under article 12.

Article 14
1. The present Protocol, of which the Chinese, English, French, Russian and Spanish texts are equally authentic, shall be deposited in the archives of the United Nations.
2. The Secretary-General of the United Nations shall transmit certified copies of the present Protocol to all States referred to in article 48 of the Covenant.

EUROPEAN CONVENTION ON HUMAN RIGHTS[4]

The Governments signatory hereto, being Members of the Council of Europe,

Considering the Universal Declaration of Human Rights proclaimed by the General Assembly of the United Nations on 10th December 1948;

Considering that this Declaration aims at securing the universal and effective recognition and observance of the Rights therein declared;

Considering that the aim of the Council of Europe is the achievement of greater unity between its Members and that one of the methods by which that aim is to be pursued is the maintenance and further realisation of Human Rights and Fundamental Freedoms;

Reaffirming their profound belief in those Fundamental Freedoms which are the foundation of justice and peace in the world and are best maintained on the one hand by an effective political democracy and on the other by a common understanding and observance of the human Rights upon which they depend;

Being resolved, as the Governments of European countries which are like-minded and have 2 common heritage Of political traditions, ideals, freedom and the rule of law, to take the first steps for the collective enforcement Of certain of the Rights stated in the Universal Declaration;

Have agreed as follows:

---

[4] In force since 3 September 1953

Article 1

The High Contracting Parties shall secure to everyone within their jurisdiction the rights and freedoms defined in Section I of this Convention.

SECTION I

Article 2

1. Everyone's right to life shall be protected by law. No one shall be deprived of his life intentionally save in the execution of a sentence of a court following his conviction of a crime for which this penalty is provided by law.

2. Deprivation of life shall not be regarded as inflicted in contravention of this Article when it results from the use of force which is no more than absolutely necessary:

   (a) in defence of any person from unlawful violence;

   (b) in order to effect a lawful arrest or to prevent the escape of a person lawfully detained;

   (c) in action lawfully taken for the purpose of quelling a riot or insurrection.

Article 3

No one shall be subjected to torture or to inhuman or degrading treatment of punishment.

Article 4

1. No one shall be held in slavery or servitude.
2. No one shall be required to perform forced or compulsory labour.
3. For the purpose of this Article the term "forced or compulsory labour" shall not include:

   (a) any work required to be done in the ordinary course of detention imposed according to the provisions of Article 5 of this Convention or during conditional release from such detention;

   (b) any service of a military character or, in case of conscientious objectors in countries where they are recognised, service exacted instead of compulsory military service;

(c) any service exacted in case of an emergency or calamity threatening the life or well-being of the community;

(d) any work or service which forms part of normal civic obligations.

Article 5

1. Everyone has the right to liberty and security of person. No one shall be deprived of his liberty save in the following cases and in accordance with a procedure prescribed by law:

   (a) the lawful detention of a person after conviction by a competent court;

   (b) the lawful arrest or detention of a person for non-compliance with the lawful order of a court or in order to secure the fulfilment of any obligation prescribed by law;

   (c) the lawful arrest or detention of 2 person effected for the purpose of bringing him before the competent legal authority on reasonable suspicion of having committed an offence or when it is reasonably considered necessary to prevent his committing an offence or fleeing after having done so;

   (d) the detention of a minor by lawful order for the purpose of educational supervision or his lawful detention for the purpose of bringing him before the competent legal authority;

   (e) the lawful detention of persons for the prevention of the spreading of infectious diseases, of persons of unsound mind, alcoholics or drug addicts or vagrants:

   (f) the lawful arrest or detention of a person to prevent his effecting an unauthorised entry into the country or of a person against whom action is being taken with a View to deportation or extradition.

2. Everyone who is arrested shall be informed promptly, in a language which he understands, of the reasons for his arrest and of any charge against him.

3. Everyone arrested or detained in accordance with the provisions of paragraph I (c) of this Article shall be brought promptly before a judge or other officer authorised by law to exercise judicial power and shall be entitled to trial within a reasonable time or to released pending trial. Release may be conditioned by guarantees to appear for trial.

4. Everyone who is deprived of his liberty by arrest or detention shall be entitled to take proceedings by which the lawfulness of his detention shall be decided speedily by a court and his release ordered if the detention is not lawful .

5. Everyone who has been the victim of arrest or detention in contravention of the provisions of this Article shall have an enforceable right to compensation.

Article 6

1. In the determination of his civil rights and Obligations or Of any criminal charge against him, everyone is entitled to a fair and public hearing within a reasonable time by in independent and impartial tribunal established by law. judgment shall be pronounced publicly but the press and public may be excluded from all or part of the trial in the interests of moral, public order or national security in a democratic society, where the interests of juveniles or the protection of the private life of the parties so require, or to the extent strictly necessary in the opinion of the court in special circumstances where publicity would prejudice the interests of justice.

2 .Everyone charged with a criminal offence shall be presumed innocent until proved guilty according to the law.

3. Everyone charged with a criminal offence has the following minimum rights:

   (a) to be informed promptly, in a language which he understands and in of the nature and cause of the accusation against him;

   (b) to have adequate time and facilities for the preparation of his defence;

   (c) to defend himself in person or through legal assistance of his own choosing or, if he his not sufficient means to pay for legal assistance, to be given it free when the interests of justice so require;

   (d) to examine or have examined witnesses against him and to obtain the attendance and examination of witnesses on his behalf under the same conditions as witnesses against him;

   (e) to have the free assistance of an interpreter if he cannot understand or speak the language used in court.

Article 7

1. No one shall be held guilty of any criminal offence on account of any of any omission which did not constitute a criminal offence under international law at the time when it was committed. Nor shall a heavier penalty be imposed than the one that was applicable at the time the criminal offence was committed.

2. This Article shall not prejudice tile trial and punishment of any person for any act or omission which, at the time when it was committed, was criminal according to the general principles of law recognised by civilised nations.

Article 8

1 Everyone has tile right to respect for his private and family life, his home and his correspondence.
2. There shall be no interference by a public authority with the exercise of this right except such as is in accordance with the law and is necessary in a democratic society in tile interests of national security, public safety or the economic well-being of the country, for the prevention of disorder or crime, for the protection of health or morals, or for the protection of the rights and freedoms of others.

Article 9

1. Everyone has the right to freedom of thought, conscience and religion; this right includes freedom to change his religion or belief and freedom, either alone or in community with others and in public or private, to manifest his religion or belief, in worship, teaching, practice and observance.
2. Freedom to manifest one's religion or beliefs shall be subject only to such limitations as are prescribed by law and are necessary in a democratic society in the interests of public safety, for the protection of public order, health or morals, or for the protection of the rights and freedoms of others.

Article 10

1 Everyone has the right to freedom of expression. This right shall include freedom to hold opinions and to receive and impart information and ideas without interference by public authority and regardless of frontiers. This Article shall not prevent States from requiring the licensing of broadcasting, television or cinema enterprises.
2. The exercise of these freedoms, since it carries with it duties and responsibilities, may be subject to such formalities, conditions, restrictions or penalties as are prescribed by law and are necessary in a democratic society, in the interest national security and territorial integrity or public safety, for prevention of disorder or crime, for the protection of health or morals, for the protection of the reputation or rights of others, for

preventing the disclosure of information received in confidence, or for maintaining the authority and impartiality of the judiciary.

Article 11

1. Everyone has the right to freedom of peaceful assembly and to freedom of association with others, including the right to form and to join trade unions for the protection of his interests.
2. No restrictions shall be placed on the exercise of these rights other than such as are prescribed by law and are necessary in a democratic society in the interests of national security or public safety, for the prevention of disorder or crime, for the protection of health or morals or for the protection of the rights and freedoms of others. This Article shall not prevent the imposition Of lawful restrictions on the exercise of these rights by members of the armed forces, of the police or of the administration of the State.

Article 12

Men and women of marriageable age have the right to marry and to found a family, according to the national laws governing the exercise of this right.

Article 13

Everyone whose rights and freedoms as set forth in this Convention are violated shall have an effective remedy before a national authority notwithstanding that the violation has been committed by persons acting in an official capacity.

Article 14

The enjoyment of the rights and freedoms set forth in this Convention shall be secured without discrimination on any ground such as sex, race, colour, language, religion, political or other opinion, national or Social origin, association with a national minority, property, birth or other status.

Article 15

1. In time of war or other public emergency threatening the life of the nation any High Contracting Party may take measures derogating from its obligations under this Convention to the extent strictly required by the exigencies of the situation, provided that such measures are not inconsistent with its other obligations under international law.

2. No derogation from Article 2, except in respect of deaths resulting from lawful acts of war, or from Articles 3, 4 (paragraph 1) and 7 shall be made under this provision.

3 Any High Contracting party availing itself of this right of derogation shall keep the Secretary-General of the Council of Europe fully informed of the measures which it has taken and the reasons therefore. It shall also inform the Secretary-General of the Council of Europe when such measures have ceased to operate and the provisions of the Convention are again being fully executed.

Article 16
Nothing in Articles 10, 11 and 14 shall be regarded as preventing the High Contracting Parties from imposing restrictions on the political activity of aliens.

Article 17
Nothing in this Convention may be interpreted as implying for any State, group or person any right to engage in any activity or perform any act aimed at the destruction of any of the rights and freedoms set forth herein or at their limitation to a greater extent than is provided for in the Convention.

Article 18
The restrictions permitted under this Convention to the raid rights and freedoms shall not be applied for any purpose other than those for which they have been prescribed.

SECTION II

Article 19
To ensure the observance of the engagements undertaken by the High Contracting Parties in the present Convention, there shall be set up:
1. A European Commission of Human Rights hereinafter referred to as "the Commission";
2. A European Court of Human Rights, hereinafter referred to 25 "the Court".

SECTION III

Article 20

The Commission shall consist of a number of members equal to that of the High Contracting Parties.　No two members Of the Commission may be nationals of the same State.

Article 21

1. The members of the Commission shall be elected by the Committee of Ministers by an absolute majority of votes, from a list of names drawn up by the Bureau of the Consultative Assembly; each group of the Representative of the High Contracting Parties in the Consultative Assembly shall put forward three candidates, of whom two at least shall be its nationals.

2. As far as applicable, the same procedure shall be followed to complete the Commission in the event of other States subsequently becoming Parties to this Convention, and in filling casual vacancies.

Article 22

1. The members of the Commission shall be elected for a Period of six years. They may be reelected.　However, of the members elected at the first election, the terms of seven members shall expire at the end of three years.

2. The members whose terms are to expire at the end of the initial period of three years shall be chosen by lot by the Secretary-General of the Council of Europe immediately after the first election has been completed.

3. In order to ensure that, as far as possible, one half of the membership of the Commission shall be renewed every three years, the Committee of Ministers may decide, before proceeding to any subsequent election, that the term or terms of office of one or more members to be elected shall be for a period other than Six years but not more than nine and not less than three years.

4. In cases where more than one term of office is involved and the Committee of Ministers applies the preceding paragraph, the allocation of the terms of office shall be effected by the drawing of lots by the Secretary-General, immediately after the election.

5. A member of the Commission elected to replace a member whose term of office has not expired shall hold office for the remainder of his predecessor's term.
6. The members of the Commission shall hold office until replaced. After having been replaced, they shall continue to deal with such cases as they already have under consideration.

Article 23
The members of the Commission shall sit on the Commission in their individual capacity.

Article 24
Any High Contracting Party may refer to the Commission, through the Secretary-General of the Council of Europe, any alleged breach of the provisions of the Convention by another High Contracting Party.

Article 25
1. The Commission may receive petitions addressed to the Secretary-General of the Council of Europe from any person, non-governmental organisation or group of individuals claiming to be the victim of a violation by one of the High Contracting Parties of the rights set forth in this Convention, provided that the High Contracting Party against which the complaint has been logged has declared that, it recognises the competence of the Commission to receive such petitions. Those of the High Contracting Parties who have made such a declaration undertake not to hinder in any way the effective exercise of this right.
2. Such declarations may be made for a specific period.
3. The declarations shall be deposited with the Secretary-General of the Council of Europe who shall transmit copies thereof to the High Contracting Parties and publish them.
4 The Commission shall only exercise the powers provided for in this Article when at least six High Contracting Parties are bound by declarations made in accordance with the preceding paragraphs.

Article 26

The Commission may only deal with the matter after all domestic remedies have been exhausted, according to the generally rccognised rules of international law, and within a period of six months from the date on which the final decision was taken.

Article 27

1. The Commission shall not deal with any petition submitted under Article 25 which
   (a) is anonymous, or
   (b) is substantially the same as a matter which has already been examined by the Commission or has already been submitted to another procedure of international investigation or settlement and if it contains no relevant new information.
2. The Commission shall consider inadmissible any petition submitted under Article 25 which it considers incompatible with the provisions of the present Convention, manifestly ill-founded, or an abuse of the right of petition.
3. The Commission shall reject any petition referred to it which it considers inadmissible under Article 26.

Article 28

In the event of the Commission accepting a petition
   (a) it shall, with a view to ascertaining the facts, undertake together with the representatives of the parties an examination of the petition and, if need, an investigation, for the effective conduct of which the States concerned shall furnish all necessary facilities, after an exchange of views with the Commission;
   (b) it shall Place itself at the disposal of the parties concerned with a view to securing a friendly settlement of the matter on the basis of respect for Human Rights as defined in this Convention.

Article 29

After it has accepted a petition submitted under Article 25, the Commission may nevertheless decide unanimously to reject the petition if, in the course of its examination, it rinds that the existence of one of the grounds for non-acceptance provided for in Article 27 has been established.

In such a case, the decision shall be communicated to the parties.

Article 30
If the Commission succeeds in effecting a friendly settlement in accordance with Article 28, it shall draw up a Report which shall be sent to the States concerned, to the Committee of Ministers and to the Secretary-General of the Council of Europe for publication. This Report shall be confined to a brief statement of the facts and of the solution reached.

Article 31
1. If a solution is not reached, the Commission shall draw up a Report on the facts and state its opinion as to whether the facts found disclose a breach by the State concerned of its obligations under the Convention. The opinions of all the members of the Commission on this point may be stated in the Report.
2. The Report shall be transmitted to the Committee of Ministers. It shall also be transmitted to the States concerned, two shall not be at liberty to publish it.
3. In transmitting the Report to the Committee of Ministers the Commission may make such proposals as it thinks fit.

Article 32
1 If the question is not referred to the Court in accordance with Article 48 of this Convention within a period of three months from the date of the transmission of the Report to the Committee of Ministers, the Committee of Ministers shall decide by a majority of two-thirds of the members entitled to sit on the Committee whether there has been a violation of the Convention,
2. In the affirmative case the Committee of Ministers shall prescribe a period during which the High Contracting Party concerned must take the measures required by the decision of the Committee of Ministers.
3. If the High Contracting Party concerned has not taken satisfactory measures within the prescribed period, the Committee of Ministers shall decide by the majority provided for in paragraph (1) above what effect shall be given to its original decision and shall publish the Report.

4. The High Contracting parties undertake to regard as binding on them any decision which the Committee of Ministers may take in application of the preceding paragraphs.

Article 33
The Commission shall meet in camera.

Article 34
Subject to the provisions of Article 29, the Commission shall take its decisions by a majority of the Members present and voting.

Article 35
The Commission shall meet as the circumstances require. The meetings shall be convened by the Secretary General of the Council of Europe.

Article 36
The Commission shall draw up its own rules of procedure.

Article 37
The secretariat of the Commission shall be provided by the Secretary General of the Council of Europe.

SECTION IV

Article 38
The European Court of Human Rights shall consist of a number of judges equal to that of the Members of the Council of Europe. No two judges may be nationals of the same State.

Article 39
1. The members of the Court shall be elected by the Consultative Assembly by a majority of the votes cast from a list of persons nominated by the Members of the Council of Europe; each Member shall nominate three candidates, of whom two at least shall be its nationals.
2. As far as applicable, the same procedure shall be followed to complete the Court in the event of the admission of new Members of the Council of Europe, and in filling casual vacancies.

3. The candidates shall be of high moral character and must either possess the qualifications required for appointment to high judicial office or be jurisconsults of recognised competence.

Article 40

1. The members of the Court shall be elected for a period of nine years. They may be re-elected. However, of the members elected at the first election the term of four members shall expire at the end of three years, and the terms of four more members shall expire at the end of six years.
2. The members whose terms are to expire at the end of the initial periods of three and six years shall be chosen by lot by the Secretary-General immediately after the first election has been completed.
3. In order to ensure that, as far as possible, one third of the membership of the court shall be renewed every three years, the Consultative Assembly may decide, before proceeding to any subsequent election, that the term or terms of office of one or more members to be elected shall be for a period other than nine years but not more than twelve and not less than six years.
4. In cases where more than one term of office is involved and the Consultative assembly applies the preceding paragraph, the allocation of the terms of office shall be effected by the drawing of lots by the Secretary-General immediately after the election.
5. A member of the Court elected to replace a member whose term of office has not expired shall hold office for the remainder of his predecessor's term
6. The members of the court shall hold office until replaced. After having been replaced, they shall continue to deal with such cases as they already have under consideration.

Article 41

The court shall elect its President and Vice-President for a period of three years. They may be re-elected.

Article 42

The members of the Court shall receive for each day of duty a compensation to be determined by the Committee of Ministers.

Article 43
For the consideration of each case brought before it the Court shall consist of a Chamber composed of seven judges. There shall sit as an ex officio member of the Chamber the judge who is a national of any State party concerned,or, if there is none, a person of its choice who shall sit in the capacity of judge: the names of the other judges shall be chosen by lot by the President before the opening of the case.

Article 44
Only the High Contracting Parties and the Commission shall have the right to bring a case before the Court.

Article 45
The jurisdiction of the Court shall extend to all cases concerning the interpretation and application of the present Convention which the High Contracting Parties or the Commission shall refer to it in accordance with Article 18.

Article 46
1. Any of the High Contracting Parties may at any time declare that it recognises as compulsory *ipso facto* and without special agreement the jurisdiction of the Court in all matters concerning the interpretation and application of the present Convention.
2. The declarations referred to above may be made unconditionally or on condition of reciprocal on the part of several or certain other High Contracting Parties or for a specified period
3. These declarations shall be deposited with the Secretary-General of the Council of Europe who shall transmit copies thereof to the High Contracting Parties

Article 47
The Court may only deal with a case after the Commission has acknowledge the failure of efforts for a friendly settlement and within the period of three months provided for in Article 32

Article 48

The following may bring a case before the Court, provided that the High Contracting Party concerned, if there is only one, or the High Contracting Parties concerned, if there is more than one, are subject to the compulsory jurisdiction of the Court or, failing that, with the consent of the High Contracting Parry concerned, if there is only one, or of the High Contracting Parties concerned if there is more than one:

    (a) the Commission;

    (b) a High Contracting Party whose national is alleged to be a victim;

    (c) a High Contracting Party which referred the case to the Commission;

    (d) a High Contracting Party against which the complaint has been lodged.

Article 49

In the event of dispute as to whether the Court has jurisdiction, the matter shall be settled by the decision of the Court.

Article 50

If the Court finds that a decision or a measure taken by a legal authority or any other authority of a High Contracting Party is completely or partially in conflict with the obligations arising from the present Convention, and if the internal law of the said Party allows only partial reparation to be made for the consequences of this decision or measure, the decision of the Court shall, if necessary, afford just satisfaction to the injured party.

Article 51

1. Reasons shall be given for the judgment of the Court.
2. If the judgment does not represent in whole or in part the unanimous opinion of the judges, any judge shall be entitled to deliver a separate opinion

Article 52

The judgment of the Court shall be final.

Article 53

The High Contracting Parties undertake to abide by the decision of the Court in any case to which they are parties

Article 54

The judgment of the Court shall be transmitted to the Committee of Ministers which shall supervise its execution.

Article 55

The Court shall draw up its own rules and shall determine its own procedure.

Article 56

1. The first election of the members of the Court shall take place after the declarations by the High Contracting Parties mentioned in Article 46 have reached a total of eight.
2. No case can be brought before the Court before this election.

SECTION V

Article 57

On receipt of a request from the Secretary General of the Council of Europe any High Contracting Party shall furnish an explanation of the manner in which its internal law ensures the effective implementation of any of the provisions of this Convention.

Article 58

The expenses of the Commission and the Court shall be borne by the Council of Europe.

Article 59

The members of the Commission and of the Court shall be entitled, during the discharge of their functions, to the privileges and immunities provided for in Article 40 of the Statute of the Council of Europe and in the agreements made thereunder.

Article 60

Nothing in this Convention shall be construed as limiting or derogating from any of the human rights and fundamental freedoms which may be ensured under the laws of any High Contracting Party or under any other agreement to which it is a Party.

Article 61
Nothing in this Convention shall prejudice the powers conferred on the Committee of Ministers by the Statute of the Council of Europe.

Article 62
The High Contracting Parties agree that, except by Special agreement, they will not avail themselves of treaties, conventions or declarations in force between them for the purpose of submitting, by way of petition, a dispute arising out of the interpretation or application of this Convention to a means of settlement other than those provided for in this Convention.

Article 63
1. Any State may at the time of its ratification or at any time thereafter declare by notification addressed to the Secretary-General of the Council of Europe that the present Convention shall extend to all or any of the territories for whose international relations it is responsible.
2. The Convention shall extend to the territory or territories named in the notification as from the thirtieth day after the receipt of this notification by the Secretary-General of the Council of Europe.
3. The provisions of this Convention shall be applied in such territories with due regard, however, to local requirements.
4. Any State which has made a declaration in accordance with paragraph I of this Article may at any time thereafter declare on behalf of one or more of the territories to which the declaration relates that it accepts the competence of the Commission to receive petitions from individuals, non-governmental organisations or groups of individuals in accordance with Article 25 of the present Convention.

Article 64
1. Any State may, when signing this Convention or when depositing its instrument of ratification, make a reservation in respect of any particular provision of the Convention to the extent that any law then in force in its territory is not in conformity with the Provision. Reservations of a general character shall not be permitted under this Article.
2. Any reservation made under this Article shall contain a brief statement of the law concerned.

Article 65

1. A High Contracting Party may denounce the present Convention only after the expiry of five years from the date on which it became a Party to it and after six months' notice contained in a notification addressed to the Secretary-General of the Council of Europe, who shall inform the other High Contracting Parties.

2. Such a denunciation shall not have the effect of releasing the High Contracting Party concerned from its obligations under this Convention in respect of any act which, being capable of constituting a violation of such obligations, may have been performed by it before the date at which the denunciation became effective.

3. Any High Contracting Party which shall cease to be a Member of the Council of Europe shall cease to be a Party to this Convention under the same conditions.

4. The Convention May be denounced in accordance with the provisions of the preceding paragraphs in respect Of any territory to which it has been declared to extend under the terms of Article 63.

Article 66

1. This Convention shall be open to the signature of the Members of the Council of Europe. It shall be ratified. Ratifications shall be deposited with the Secretary-General of the Council of Europe.

2. The present Convention shall come into force after the deposit of ten instruments of ratification.

3. As regards any signatory ratifying subsequently, the Convention shall come into force at the date of tile deposit of its instrument of ratification.

4. The Secretary-General of the Council of Europe shall notify all the Members of the Council of Europe of the entry into force of the Convention, the names of the High Contracting Parties who have ratified it, and the deposit of all instruments Of ratification which May be affected subsequently.

Done at Rome this 4th day of November 1950 in English and French, both texts being equally authentic, in a single copy which shall remain deposited in the archives of the Council of Europe. The Secretary General shall transmit certified copies to each of the signatories.

ADDITIONAL PROTOCOLS[5]

PROTOCOL (NO. 1) TO THE CONVENTION FOR THE PROTECTION OF HUMAN RIGHTS AND FUNDAMENTAL FREEDOMS[6]

The Governments signatory hereto, being Members of the Council of Europe,
Being resolved to take steps to ensure the collective enforcement of certain rights and freedoms other than those already included in Section I of the Convention for the Protection of Human Rights and Fundamental Freedoms signed at Rome on 4th November, 1950 (hereinafter referred to as "the Convention"),
Have agreed as follows:

Article 1
Every natural or legal person is entitled to the peaceful enjoyment of his possessions. No one shall be deprived of his possessions except in the public interest and subject to the conditions provided for by law and by the general principles of international law.
The preceding provisions shall not, however, in any way impair the right of a State to enforce such laws as it deems necessary to control the use of property in accordance with the general interest or to secure the payment of taxes or other contributions or penalties.

Article 2
No person shall be denied the right to education. In the exercise Of any functions which it assumes in relation to education and to teaching, the State shall respect the right of parents to ensure such education and teaching in conformity with their own religious and philosophical convictions.

---

[5] Protocols 3, 5 and 8 concern amendments to the text of the Convention on Human Rights and have already been incorporated into the text printed here, with the exception of Protocol No. 8 which is not yet in force.

[6] In force since 18 May 1954.

Article 3

The High Contracting Parties undertake to hold free elections at reasonable intervals by secret ballot, under conditions which will ensure the free expression of the opinion of the people in the choice of the legislature.

Article 4

Any High Contracting Party may at the time of signature or ratification or at any time thereafter communicate to the Secretary-General of the Council of Europe a declaration stating the extent to which it undertakes that the provisions of the present Protocol shall apply to such of the territories the international relations of which it is responsible as are named therein.

Any High Contracting Party which has communicated a declaration in virtue of the preceding paragraph may from time to time communicate a further declaration modifying the terms of any former declaration or terminating the application of the provisions of this Protocol in respect Of any territory.

A declaration made in accordance with this Article shall be deemed to have been made in accordance with Paragraph (1) of Article 63 of the Convention.

Article 5

As between the High Contracting Parties the provisions of Articles 1, 2, 3 and 4 of this Protocol shall be regarded 25 additional Articles to the Convention and all the provisions of the Convention shall apply accordingly.

Article 6

This Protocol shall be open for signature by the Members of the Council of Europe, who are the signatories of the Convention; it shall be ratified at the same time as of after the ratification of the Convention. It shall enter into force after the deposit of ten instruments of ratification. As regards any signatory ratifying subsequently, the Protocol shall enter into force at the date of the deposit of its instrument of ratification.

The instruments of ratification shall be deposited with the Secretary-General of the Council of Europe, who will notify all Members of the names of those who have ratified.

Done at Paris on the 20th day of March 1952, in English and French, both texts being equally authentic, in a single copy which shall remain deposited in the archives of the Council of Europe. The Secretary General shall transmit certified copies to each of the signatory Governments.

PROTOCOL NO. 2 TO THE CONVENTION FOR THE PROTECTION OF HUMAN RIGHTS AND FUNDAMENTAL FREEDOMS CONFERRING UPON THE EUROPEAN COURT OF HUMAN RIGHTS COMPETENCE TO GIVE ADVISORY OPINIONS[7]

The member States of the Council of Europe signatory hereto:

Having regard to the provisions of the Convention for the Protection of Human Rights and Fundamental Freedoms signed at Rome on 4th November 1950 (hereinafter referred to as "the Convention") and, in particular, Article 19 instituting, among other bodies, a European Court of Human Rights (hereinafter referred to as "the Court");

Considering that it is expedient to confer upon the Court competence to give advisory opinions subject to certain conditions;

Have agreed as follows:

Article 1

1. The Court may, at the request of the Committee of Ministers, give advisory opinions on legal questions concerning the interpretation of the Convention and the Protocols thereto.

2. Such opinions shall not deal with any question relating to the content or scope of the rights or freedoms derived in Section I of the Convention and in the Protocols thereto, or with any other question which the Commission, the Court or the Committee of Ministers might have to consider in consequence of any such proceedings as could be instituted in accordance with the Convention.

3. Decisions of the Committee of Ministers to request an advisory opinion of the Court shall require a two-thirds majority vote of the representatives entitled to sit on the Committee.

Article 2

The Court shall decide whether a request for an advisory opinion submitted by the Committee of Ministers is within its consultative competence as defined in Article I of this Protocol.

---

[7] In force since 21 September 1970.

Article 3

1. For the consideration of requests for an advisory opinion, the Court shall sit in plenary session.
2. Reasons shall be given for advisory opinions of the Court.
3. If the advisory opinion does not represent in whole or in part the unanimous opinion of the judges, any judge shall be entitled to deliver a separate opinion.
4. Advisory opinions of the Court shall be communicated to the Committee of Ministers.

Article 4

The powers of the Court under Article 55 of the Convention shall extend to the drawing up of such rules and the determination of such procedure as the Court may think necessary for the purposes of this Protocol.

Article 5

1. This Protocol shall be open to signature by member States of the Council of Europe, signatories to the Convention, who may become Parties to it by:
   (a) signature without reservation in respect of ratification or acceptance: Protocol No. 4
   (b) signature with reservation in respect of ratification or acceptance, followed by ratification of acceptance.
   Instruments of ratification or acceptance shall be deposited with the Secretary-General of the Council of Europe.
2. This Protocol shall enter into force as soon as all States Parties to the Convention shall have become Parties to the Protocol, in accordance with the provisions of paragraph 1 of this Article.
3. From the date of the entry into force of this Protocol, Articles 1 to 4 shall be considered an integral part of the Convention.
4. The Secretary-General of the Council of Europe shall notify the member States of the Council of:
   (a) any signature without reservation in respect of ratification or acceptance;
   (b) any signature with reservation in respect of ratification of acceptance;
   (c) the deposit of any instrument of ratification or acceptance;
   (d) the date of entry into force of this Protocol in accordance with paragraph 2 of this Article.

In witness whereof, the undersigned, being duly authorised thereto, have signed this Protocol.

Done at Strasbourg, this 6th day of May 1963, in English and French, both texts being equally authoritative, in a single copy which shall remain deposited in the archives of the Council of Europe. The Secretary General shall transmit certified copies to each of the signatory States.

PROTOCOL NO. 4 TO THE CONVENTION FOR THE PROTECTION OF HUMAN RIGHTS AND FUNDAMENTAL FREEDOMS, SECURING CERTAIN RIGHTS AND FREEDOMS OTHER THAN THOSE ALREADY INCLUDED IN THE CONVENTION AND IN THE FIRST PROTOCOL THERETO[8]

The Governments signatory hereto, being Members of the Council of Europe,

Being resolved to take steps to ensure the collective enforcement of certain rights and freedoms other than those already included in Section I of the Convention for the Protection of Human Rights and Fundamental Freedoms signed at Rome on 4th November, 1950 (hereinafter referred to as "the Convention") and in Articles I to 3 of the First Protocol to the Convention, signed at Paris on 20th March, 1952,

Have agreed as follows:

Article 1
No one shall be deprived of his liberty merely on the ground of inability to fulfil a contractual obligation.

Article 2
1. Everyone lawfully within the territory of a State shall, within that territory have the right to liberty of movement and freedom to choose his residence.
2. Everyone shall be free to leave any country, including his own.
3. No restrictions shall be placed on the exercise of these rights other than such as are in accordance with law and are necessary in a democratic society in the interests of national security or public safety, for the maintenance of "ordre public", for the prevention of crime, for the protection of health or morals, or for the protection of the rights and freedoms of others.

---

[8] In force since 2 May 1968.

4. The rights set forth in paragraph 1 may also be subject, in particular areas, to restrictions imposed in accordance with law and justified by the public interest in a democratic society.

Article 3
1. No one shall be expelled, by means either of an individual or of a collective measure, from the territory of the State of which he is a national.
2. No one shall be deprived of the right to enter the territory of the State of which he is a national.

Article 4
Collective expulsion of aliens is prohibited.

Article 5
1. Any High Contracting Party may, at the time of signature or ratification of this Protocol, or at any time thereafter, communicate to the Secretary-General of the Council of Europe a declaration stating the extent to which it undertakes that the provisions of this Protocol shall apply to such of the territories for the international relations of which it is responsible as are named therein.
2. Any High Contracting Party which has communicated a declaration in virtue of the preceding paragraph may, from time to time, communicate a further declaration modifying the terms of any former declaration or terminating the application of the provisions of this Protocol in respect Of any territory.
3. A declaration made in accordance with this Article shall be deemed to have been made in accordance with paragraph 1 of Article 63 of the Convention.
4. The territory Of any State to which this Protocol applies by virtue of ratification or acceptance by that State, and each territory to which this Protocol is applied by virtue of a declaration by that State under this Article, shall be treated as separate territories for the purpose of the references in Articles 2 and 3 to the territory of a State.

Article 6

1. As between the High Contracting Parties the provisions of Articles 1 to 5 of this Protocol shall be regarded as additional Articles to the Convention, and all the provisions of the Convention shall apply accordingly.
2. Nevertheless, the right of individual recourse recognised by a declaration made under Article 25 of the Convention, or the acceptance of the compulsory jurisdiction of the Court by a declaration made under Article 46 of the Convention, shall not be effective in relation to this Protocol unless the High Contracting Party concerned has made a statement recognising such right, or accepting such jurisdiction, in respect of all or any of Articles 1 to 4 of the Protocol.

Article 7

1. This Protocol shall be open for signature by the Members of the Council of Europe who are the signatories of the Convention; it shall be ratified at the same time as or after the ratification of the Convention. It shall enter into force after the deposit of five instruments of ratification. As regards any signatory ratifying subsequently the Protocol shall enter into force at the date of the deposit of its instrument of ratification.
2. The instruments of ratification shall be deposited with the Secretary General of the Council of Europe, who will notify all Members of the names of those who have ratified.

In witness whereof, the undersigned, being duly authorised thereto, have signed this Protocol.

Done at Strasbourg, this 16th day of September 1963, in English and in French, both texts being equally authoritative, in a single copy which shall remain deposited in the archives of the Council of Europe. The Secretary General shall transmit certified copies to each of the signatory States.

PROTOCOL NO. 6 TO THE CONVENTION FOR THE PROTECTION OF HUMAN RIGHTS AND FUNDAMENTAL FREEDOMS CONCERNING THE ABOLITION OF THE DEATH PENALTY[9]

The member States of the Council of Europe, signatory to this Protocol to the Convention for the Protection of Human Rights and Fundamental Freedoms,

---

[9] In force since 1 March 1985.

signed at Rome on 4 November 1950 (hereinafter referred to as "the Convention"),
Considering that the evolution that has occurred in several member States of the Council of Europe expresses a general tendency in favour of abolition of the death penalty,
Have agreed as follows:

Article 1
The death penalty shall be abolished. No one shall be condemned to such penalty or executed.

Article 2
A State may make provision in its law for the death penalty in respect of acts committed in time of war or of imminent threat of war; such penalty shall be applied only in the instances laid down in the law and in accordance with its provisions. The State shall communicate to the Secretary General Of the Council of Europe the relevant provisions of that law.

Article 3
No derogation from the provisions of this Protocol shall be made under Article 15 of the Convention.

Article 4
No reservation may be made under Article 64 of the Convention in respect of the provisions of this Protocol.

Article 5
1. Any State may at the time of signature or when depositing its instrument of ratification, acceptance or approval, specify the territory or territories to which this Protocol shall apply.
2. Any State may at any later date, by a declaration addressed to the Secretary General of the Council of Europe, extend the application of this Protocol to any other territory specified in the declaration. In respect of such territory the Protocol shall enter into force on the first day of the month following the date of receipt of such a declaration by the Secretary General.

3. Any declaration made under the two preceding paragraphs may, in respect of any territory specified in such declaration, be withdrawn by a notification addressed to the Secretary General. The withdrawal shall become effective on the first day of the month following the date of receipt of such notification by the secretary General.

Article 6

As between the States Parties the provisions of Articles 1 to 5 of this Protocol shall be regarded as additional articles to the Convention and all the provisions of the Convention shall apply accordingly.

Article 7

This Protocol shall be open for signature by the member States of the Council of Europe, signatories to the Convention. It shall be subject to ratification, acceptance or approval. A member State of the Council of Europe may not ratify, accept or approve this Protocol unless it has, simultaneously or previously, ratified the Convention. Instruments of ratification, acceptance or approval shall be deposited with the Secretary General of the Council of Europe.

Article 8

1. This Protocol shall enter into force on the first day of the month following the date on which five member States of the Council of Europe have expressed their consent to be bound by the Protocol in accordance with the provisions of Article 7.
2. In respect of any member State which subsequently expresses its consent to be bound by it, the Protocol shall enter into force on the first day of the month following the date of the deposit of the instrument of ratification, acceptance or approval.

Article 9

The Secretary General of the Council of Europe shall notify the member States of the Council of:
   (a) any signature;
   (b) the deposit of any instrument of ratification, acceptance or approval;
   (c) any date of entry into force of this Protocol in accordance with Article 5 and 8;

(d) any other act, notification or communication relating to this Protocol.

In witness whereof the undersigned, being duly authorised thereto, have signed this Protocol.

Done at Strasbourg, the twenty-eighth April one thousand nine hundred and eighty-three, in English and French, both texts being equally authentic, in a single copy which shall be deposited in the archives of the Council of Europe. The Secretary General of the Council of Europe shall transmit certified copies to each member State of the Council of Europa.

PROTOCOL NO. 7 TO THE CONVENTION FOR THE PROTECTION OF HUMAN RIGHTS AND FUNDAMENTAL FREEDOMS[10]

The member States of the Council of Europe signatory hereto,

Being resolved to take further steps to ensure the collective enforcement of certain rights and freedoms by means of the Convention for the Protection of Human Rights and Fundamental Freedoms signed at Rome on 4 November 1950 (hereinafter referred to as "the Convention");

Have agreed as follows:

Article 1

1 An alien lawfully resident in the territory of a State shall not be expelled therefrom except in pursuance of a decision reached in accordance with law and shall be allowed:

(a) to submit reasons against his expulsion,

(b) to have his case reviewed, and

(c) to be represented for these purposes before the competent authority or a person or persons designated by that authority.

2 An alien may be expelled before the exercise of his rights under Paragraph 1 (2), (b) and (c) of this Article, when such expulsion is necessary in the interests of public order or is grounded on reasons of national security.

Article 2

1. Everyone convicted of a criminal offence by a tribunal shall have the right to have conviction or sentence reviewed by a higher tribunal. The exercise

---

[10] I force since March 1, 1985

of this right, including the grounds on which it may be exercised, shall be governed by law.

2. This right may be subject to exceptions in regard to offences of a minor character, as prescribed by law, or in cases in which the person concerned was tried in the first instance by the highest tribunal or was convicted following an appeal against acquittals

Article 3

When a person has by a final decision been convicted of a criminal offence and when subsequently his conviction has been reversed, or lie has been pardoned, on the ground that a new or newly discovered fact shows conclusively that there has been a miscarriage of justice, the person who has suffered punishment as a result of such conviction shall be compensated according to the law or the practice of the State concerned, unless it is proved that the non-disclosure of the unknown fact in time is wholly or partly attributable to him.

Article 4

1. No one shall be liable to be tried or punished again in criminal proceedings under the jurisdiction of the same State for an offence for which he has already been finally acquitted or convicted in accordance with the law and penal procedure of that State.

2. The provisions of the preceding paragraph shall not prevent the reopening of the case in accordance with the law and penal procedure of the State concerned, if there is evidence of new or newly discovered facts, or if there has been a fundamental defect in the previous proceedings, which could affect the outcome of the case.

3. No derogation from this Article shall be made under Article 15 of the Convention.

Article 5

1. Spouses shall enjoy equality of rights and responsibilities of a private law character between them, and in their relations with their children, as to marriage, during marriage and in the event of its dissolution. This Article shall not prevent States from taking such measures as are necessary in the interests of the children.

Article 6

1. Any State May at the time of signature or when depositing its instrument of ratification, acceptance or approval, specify the territory or territories to which this Protocol shall apply and State the extent to which it undertakes that the provisions of this Protocol shall apply to this or these territories.

2. Any State may at any later date, by a declaration addressed to the Secretary General of the Council of Europe, extend the application of this Protocol to any other territory specified in the declaration. In respect of such territory the Protocol shall enter into force on the first day of the month following the expiration of a period of two months after the date of receipt by the Secretary General of such declaration.

3. Any declaration made under the two preceding paragraphs may, in respect of any territory specified in such declaration, be withdrawn or modified by a notification addressed to the Secretary General. The withdrawal or modification shall become effective on the first day of the month following the expiration of a period of two months after the date of receipt of such notification by the Secretary General.

4. A declaration made in accordance with this Article shall be deemed to have been made in accordance with paragraph 1 of Article 63 of the Convention

5. The territory of any State to which this Protocol applies by virtue of ratification, acceptance or approval by that State, and each territory to which this Protocol is applied by virtue of a declaration by that State under this Article, may be treated as separate territories for the purpose of the reference in Article 1 to the territory of a State.

Article 7

1. As between the States Parties, the provisions of Articles 1 to 6 of this Protocol shall be regarded as additional Articles to the Convention, and all the previsions of the Convention shall apply accordingly.

2. Nevertheless, the right of individual recourse recognised by a declaration made under Article 25 of the Convention, or the acceptance of the compulsory jurisdiction of the Court by a declaration made under Article 46 of the Convention, shall not be effective in relation to this Protocol unless the State concerned has made a statement recognising such right, or accepting such jurisdiction in respect of Articles 1 to 5 of this Protocol.

Article 8

This Protocol shall be open for signature by member States of the Council of Europe which have signed the Convention. It is subject to ratification, acceptance or approval. member State of the Council of Europe may not ratify, accept or approve this Protocol without previously or simultaneously ratifying the Convention. Instruments of ratification, acceptance or approval shall be deposited with the Secretary General of the Council of Europe.

Article 9

1. This Protocol shall enter into force on the first day of the month following the expiration of a period of two months after the date on which seven member States of the Council of Europe have expressed their consent to be bound by the Protocol in accordance with the provisions of Article 8.
2. In respect of any member State which subsequently expresses its consent to be bound by it, the Protocol shall enter into force on the first day of the month following the expiration of a period of two months after the date of the deposit of the instrument of ratification, acceptance or approval.

Article 10

The Secretary General of the Council of Europe shall notify all the member States of the Council of:.

  (a) any signature;
  (b) the deposit of any instrument of ratification, acceptance or approval;
  (c) any date of entry into force of this Protocol in accordance with Article 6 and 9;
  (d) any other act, notification or declaration relating to this Protocol.

In witness whereof the undersigned, being duly authorised thereto, have signed this Protocol.

Done at Strasbourg, the twenty-two November one thousand nine hundred and eighty four, in English and French, both texts being equally authentic, in a single copy which shall be deposited in the archives of the Council of Europe shall transmit certified copies to each member State of the Council.

AMERICAN CONVENTION ON HUMAN RIGHTS [11]

PREAMBLE

The American states signatory to the present Convention,

Reaffirming their intention to consolidate in this hemisphere, within the framework of democratic institutions, a system of personal liberty and social justice based on respect for the essential rights of man;

Recognizing that the essential rights of man are not derived from one's being a national of a certain state, but are based upon attributes of the human personality, and that they therefore justify international protection in the form of a convention reinforcing or complementing the protection provided by the domestic law of the American states;

Considering that these principles have been set forth in the Charter of the Organization of American States, in the American Declaration of the Rights and Duties of Man, and in the Universal Declaration of Human Rights, and that they have been reaffirmed and refined in other international instruments, worldwide as well as regional in scope;

Reiterating that, in accordance with the Universal Declaration of Human Rights, the ideal of free men enjoying freedom from fear and want can be achieved only if conditions are created whereby everyone may enjoy his economic, social, and cultural rights, as well as his Civil and political rights; and

Considering that the Third Special Inter-American Conference (Buenos Aires, 1967) approved the incorporation into the Charter of the Organization itself of broader standards with respect to economic, Social, and educational rights and resolved that an inter-American convention on human rights should determine the structure, competence, and procedure of the organs responsible for these matters,

Have agreed upon the following:

---

[11] In force since 18 July 1978.

PART I. STATE OBLIGATIONS AND RIGHTS PROTECTED

CHAPTER I. GENERAL OBLIGATIONS

Article 1. Obligation to Respect Rights

1. The States Parties to this Convention undertake to respect the rights and freedoms recognized herein and to ensure to all persons subject to their jurisdiction the free and full exercise of those rights and freedoms, without any discrimination for reasons of race, color, Sex, language, religion, political or other opinion, national of social origin, economic status, birth, or any other social condition.
2. For the purposes of this Convention, "person" means every human being.

Article 2 Domestic Legal Effects

Where the exercise Of any of the rights or freedoms referred to in Article I is not already ensured by legislative or other provisions, the States Parties undertake to adopt, in accordance with their constitutional processes and the provisions of this Convention, such legislative or other measures as may be necessary to give effect to those rights of freedoms.

CHAPTER II. CIVIL AND POLITICAL RIGHTS

Article 3. Right to juridical Personality

Every person has the right to recognition as a person before the law.

Article 4. Right to Life

1. Every person has the right to have his life respected. This right shall be protected by law and, in general, from the moment of conception. No one shall be arbitrarily deprived of his life.
2. In countries that have not abolished the death penalty, it may be imposed only for the most serious crimes and pursuant to a final judgment rendered by a competent court and in accordance with a law establishing such punishment, enacted prior to the commission of the crime. The application of such punishment shall not be extended to crimes to which it does not presently apply.

3. The death penalty shall not be reestablished in States that have abolished it.

4. In no case shall Capital punishment be inflicted for political offenses or related common crimes.

5. Capital punishment shall not be imposed upon persons who, at the time the crime was committed, were under 18 years of age or over 70 years of age; nor shall it be applied to pregnant women.

6. Every person condemned to death shall have the right to apply for amnesty, pardon, or commutation of sentence. which may be granted in all cases. Capital punishment shall not be imposed while such a petition is pending decision by the competent authority.

Article 5. Right to Humane Treatment

1. Every person has the right to have his physical, mental, and moral integrity respected.

2. No one shall be subjected to torture or to cruel, inhuman, or degrading punishment or treatment. All persons deprived of their liberty shall be treated with respect for the inherent dignity of the human person.

3. Punishment shall not be extended to any person other than the criminal.

4. Accused persons shall, save in exceptional circumstances, be segregated from convicted persons, and shall be subject to separate treatment appropriate to their Status as unconvicted persons.

5. Minors while subject to criminal proceedings shall be separated from adults and brought before specialized tribunals, as speedily as possible, so that they may be treated in accordance with their Status as minors.

6. Punishments consisting of deprivation of liberty shall have as an essential aim the reform and social re-adaptation of the prisoners.

Article 6. Freedom from Slavery

1. No one shall be subject to slavery or to involuntary servitude, which are prohibited in all their forms, as are the slave trade and traffic in women.

2. No one shall be required to perform forced of compulsory labor. This provision shall not be interpreted to mean that, in those countries in which the penalty established for certain crimes is deprivation of liberty at forced labor, the carrying out of such a sentence imposed by a competent court is prohibited. Forced labor shall not adversely affect the dignity or the physical or intellectual capacity of the prisoner.

3. For the purposes of this article, the following do not constitute forced or compulsory labor:
   a) work or service normally required of a person imprisoned in execution of a sentence or formal decision passed by the competent judicial authority. Such work or service shall be carried out under the supervision and control of public authorities, and any persons performing such work or service shall not be placed at the disposal of any private party, company, or juridical person;
   b) military service and, in countries in which conscientious objectors are recognized, national service that the law may provide for in lieu of military service;
   (c) service exacted in time of danger or calamity that threatens the existence or the well-being of the community; or
   (d) work or service that forms part of normal civic obligations.

Article 7. Right to Personal Liberty

1. Every person shall the right to personal liberty and security.
2. No one shall be deprived of his physical liberty except for the reasons and under the conditions established beforehand by the constitution of the State Party concerned or by a law established pursuant thereto.
3. No one shall be subject to arbitrary arrest or imprisonment.
4. Anyone who is detained shall be informed of the reasons for his detention and shall be promptly notified of the charge or charges against him.
5 Any person detained shall be brought promptly before a judge or other officer authorized by law to exercise judicial power and shall be entitled to trial within a reasonable time or to be released without prejudice to the continuation of the proceedings. His release may be subject to guarantees to assure his appearance for trial.
6 Anyone who is deprived of his liberty shall be entitled to recourse to a competent court, in order that the court may decide without delay on tile lawfulness of his arrest or detention and order his release if the arrest or detention is unlawful. In States Parties whose laws provide that anyone who believes himself to be threatened with deprivation of his liberty is entitled to recourse to a competent court in order that it may decide on tile lawfulness of such threat, this remedy may not be restricted or abolished. The interested party or another person in his behalf is entitled to seek these remedies.

7 No one shall be detained for debt. This principle shall not limit the orders of a competent judicial authority issued for non-fulfillment of duties of support.

Article 8. Right to a Fair Trial

1. Every person has the right to a hearing, with due guarantees and within a reasonable time, by a competent, independent, and impartial tribunal, previously established by law, in the substantiation of any accusation of a criminal nature made :against him or for the determination of his rights and obligations of a civil, labor, fiscal, or any other nature.

2 Every person accused of a criminal offense has the right to be presumed innocent so long as his guilt has not been proven according to law. During the proceedings, every person is entitled, with full equality, to the following minimum guarantees:

(a) the right of the accused to be assisted without charge by a translator or interpreter, if he does not understand or does not speak the language of the tribunal or court;

(b) prior notification in detail to the accused of the charges against him;

(c) adequate time and means for the preparation of his defense;

(d) the right of the accused to defend himself personally or to be assisted by legal counsel of his own choosing, and to communicate freely and privately with his counsel;

(e) the inalienable right to be assisted by counsel provided by the state, paid or not as the domestic law provides, if the accused does not defend himself personally or engage his own counsel within the time period established by law;

(f) the right of the defense to examine witnesses present in the court and to obtain the appearance, as witnesses, of experts or other persons who may throw light on the facts;

(g) the right not to be compelled to be a witness against himself or to plead guilty; and

(h) the right to appeal tire judgment to a higher court.

3. A confession of guilt by the accused shall be valid only if it is made without coercion of any kind.

4. An accused person acquitted by a non-applicable judgment shall not be subjected to a new trial for the same cause.

5. Criminal proceedings shall be public, except insofar as may be necessary to protect the interests of justice.

Article 9. Freedom from Ex Post Facto Laws

No one shall be convicted of any act or omission that did not constitute a criminal offense, under the applicable law, at the time it was committed. A heavier penalty shall not be imposed than the one that was applicable at the time the criminal offense was committed. If subsequent to the commission of the offense the law provides for the imposition of a lighter punishment, the guilty person shall benefit therefrom.

Article 10. Right to Compensation

Every person has the right to be compensated in accordance with the law in the event he has been sentenced by a final judgment through a miscarriage of justice.

Article 11. Right to Privacy

1. Everyone has the right to have his honor respected and his dignity recognized.
2. No one may be the object of arbitrary or abusive interference with his private life, his family, his home, or his correspondence, or of unlawful attacks on his honor or reputation.
3. Everyone has the right to the protection of the law against such interference or attacks.

Article 12. Freedom of Conscience and Religion

1. Everyone has the right to freedom of conscience and of religion. This right includes freedom to maintain or to change one's religion or beliefs, and freedom to profess or disseminate one's religion or beliefs, either individually or together with others in public or in private.
2. No one shall be subject to restrictions that might impair his freedom to maintain or to change his religion or belief.
3. Freedom to manifest one's religion and beliefs may be subject only to the limitations prescribed by law that are necessary to protect public safety, order, health, or morals, or the rights or freedoms of others.

4. Parents or guardians, as the case may be, have the right to provide for the religious and moral education of their children or wards that is in accord with their own convictions.

Article 13. Freedom of Though and Expression
1. Everyone has the right to freedom of thought and expression. This right includes freedom to seek, receive, and impart information and ideas of, all kinds, regardless of frontiers, either orally, in writing, in print, in the form of art, or through any other medium of one's choice.
2. The exercise of the right provided for in the foregoing paragraph shall not be subject to prior censorship but shall be subject to subsequent impo.sitioii of liability, which shall be expressly established by law to the extent necessary to ensure:
   (a) respect for the rights or reputations of others; or
   (b) the protection of national security, public order, or public health or morals.
3. The right of expression may not be restricted by indirect methods or means, such as the abuse of government or private controls over newsprint, radio broadcasting frequencies, or equipment used in the dissemination of information, or by any other means tending to impede the communication and circulation of ideas and opinions.
4. Notwithstanding the provisions of paragraph 2 above, public entertainment may be subject by law to prior censorship for the sole purpose of regulating access to them for the moral protection of childhood and adolescence.
5. Any propaganda for war and any advocacy of national, racial, or religious hatred that constitute incitements to lawless violence or to any other similar illegal action against any person or group of persons on any grounds including those of race, color, religion, language, or national origin shall be considered as offenses punishable by law.

Article 14. Right of Reply
1. Anyone injured by inaccurate or offensive statements or ideas disseminated to the public in general by a legally regulated medium of communication has the right to reply or to make a correction using the same communications outlet, under such conditions as the law may establish.

2. The correction or reply shall not in any case remit other legal liabilities that may have been incurred.
3. For the effective protection of honor and reputation, every publisher, and every newspaper, motion picture. radio, and television company, shall have a person responsible who is not protected by immunities or special privileges.

Article 15. Right of Assembly

The right of peaceful assembly, without arms, is recognized. No restrictions may be placed on the exercise of this right other than those imposed in conformity with the law and necessary in a democratic society in the interest of national security, public safety or public order, or to protect public health or morals or the rights or freedoms of others.

Article 16. Freedom of Association

1. Everyone has the right to associate freely for ideological, religious, political, economic, labor, social, cultural, Sports, or other purposes.
2. The exercise of this right shall be subject only to such restrictions established by law as may be necessary in a democratic society, in the interest of national security, public safety or public order, or to protect public health or moral or the rights and freedoms of others.
3. The provisions of this article do not bar the imposition of legal restrictions, including even deprivation of the exercise of the right Of association, on members of the armed forces and the police.

Article 17. Rights of the Family

1. The family is the natural and fundamental group unit of society and is entitled to protection by society and the state.
2. The right of men and women of marriageable age to marry and to raise a family shall be recognized, if they meet the conditions required by domestic laws insofar as such conditions do not affect the principle of nondiscrimination established in this Convention.
3. No marriage shall be entered into without the free and full consent of the intending spouses.
4. The States parties shall take appropriate steps to ensure the equality of rights and the adequate balancing of responsibilities of the spouses as to marriage, during marriage, and in the event of its dissolution. In case of

dissolution, provision shall be made for the necessary protection of any children solely on the basis of their own best interests.

5. The law shall recognize equal rights for children born out of wedlock and those born in wedlock.

Article 18. Right to a Name
Every person has the right to a given name and to the surnames of his parents or that of one of them. The law shall regulate the manner in which this right shall he ensured for all, by the use of assumed names if necessary.

Article 19. Rights of the Child
Every minor child has the right to the measures of protection required by his condition as a minor on the part of his family, society, and the state.

Article 20 Right to Nationality
1. Every person has the right to a nationality.
2. Every person has the right to the nationality of the state in whose territory he was born if he does not have the right to any other nationality.
3. No one shall be arbitrarily deprived of his nationality or of the right to change it.

Article 21. Right to Property
1. Everyone has the right to the use and enjoyment of his property. The law may be subordinate such use and enjoyment to the interest of society.
2. No one shall be deprived of his property except upon payment of just compensation, for reasons of public utility or social interest, and in the cases and according to the forms established by law.
3. Usury and any other form of exploitation of man by man shall be prohibited by law.

Article 22. Freedom of Movement and Residence
1. Every person lawfully in the territory of a State Party has the right to move about in it, and to reside in it subject to the provisions of the law.
2. Every person has the right to leave any country freely, including his own.
3. The exercise of the foregoing rights may be restricted only pursuant to a law to the extent necessary in a democratic society to prevent crime or to

protect national security, public safety, public order, public morals, public health, or the rights or freedoms of others.

4. The exercise of the rights recognized in paragraph 1 may also be restricted by law in designated zones for reasons of public interest.

5. No one can be expelled from the territory of the state of which he is a national or be deprived of the right to enter it.

6. An alien lawfully in the territory of a State Party to this Convention may be expelled from it only pursuant to a decision reached in accordance with the law.

7. Every person has the right to seek and be granted asylum in a foreign territory, in accordance with the legislation of the state and international conventions, in the event lie is being pursued for political offenses or related common crimes.

8. In no case may an alien be deported or returned to a country, regardless of whether or not it is his country of origin, if in that country his right to life or personal freedom is in danger of being violated because of his race, nationality, religion, social status, or political opinions.

9. The collective expulsion of aliens is prohibited.

Article 23. Right to Participate on Government

1. Every citizen shall enjoy the following rights and opportunities:
   (a) to take part in the conduct of public affairs, directly or through freely chosen representatives;
   (b) to Vote and to be elected in genuine periodic elections, which shall be by universal and equal suffrage and by secret ballot that guarantees the free expression of the will of the voters; and
   (c) to have access, under general conditions of equality, to the public service of his country.

2. The law may regulate the exercise of the rights and opportunities referred to in the preceding paragraph only on the basis Of age, nationality, residence, language, education, civil and mental capacity, or sentencing by a competent court in criminal proceedings.

Article 24. Right to Equal Protection

All persons are equal before the law. Consequently, they are entitled, without discrimination, to equal protection of the law.

Article 25. Right to Judicial Protection
1. Everyone has the right to simple and prompt recourse, or any other effective recourse, to a competent court or tribunal for protection against acts that violate his fundamental rights recognized by the constitution or laws of the state concerned or by this Convention, even though such violation may have been committed by persons acting in the course of their official duties.
2. The States Parties undertake:
    (a) to ensure that any person claiming such remedy shall have his rights determined by the competent authority provided for by the legal system of the state;
    (b) to develop the possibilities of judicial remedy; and
    (c) to ensure that the comment authorities shall enforce such remedies when granted.

CHAPTER III. ECONOMIC, SOCIAL, AND CULTURAL RIGHTS

Article 26. Progressive Development
The States Parties undertake to adopt measures, both internally and through international cooperation, especially those of an economic and technical nature, with a view to achieving progressively, by legislation or other appropriate means, the full realization of the rights implicit in the economic, social, educational, scientific, and cultural standards set forth in the Charter of the Organization of American States as amended by the Protocol of Buenos Aires.

CHAPTER IV. SUSPENSION OF GUARANTEES, INTERPRETATION, AND APPLICATION

Article 27. Suspension of Guarantees
1. In time of war, public danger, or other emergency that threatens the independence or security of a State Party, it may take measures derogating from its obligations under the present Convention to the extent and for the period of time strictly required by the exigencies of the situation, provided that such measures are not inconsistent with its other obligations under international law and do not involve discrimination on the ground of race, color, sex, language, religion, or social origin.

2. The foregoing provision does not authorize any suspension of the following articles: Article 3 (Right to Juridical Personality), Article 4 (Right to Life), Article 5 (Right to Humane Treatment), Article 6 (Freedom from Slavery), Article 9 (Freedom from *Ex Post Facto* Laws), Article 12 (Freedom of Conscience and Religion), Article 17 (Rights of the Family), Article 18 (Right to a Name), Article 19 (Rights of the Child), Article 20 (Right to Nationality), and Article 23 (Right to Participate in Government), or of the judicial guarantees essential for the protection of such rights.

3. Any State Party availing itself of the right of suspension shall immediately inform the other States Parties, through the Secretary General of the Organization of American States, of the provisions the application of which it has suspended, the reasons that gave rise to the suspension, and the date set for the termination of such suspension.

Article 28. Federal Clause

1. Where a State Party is constituted as a federal State, the national government of such State Party shall implement all the provisions of the Convention over whose subject matter it exercises legislative and judicial jurisdiction.

2. With respect to the provisions over whose subject matter the constituent units of the federal State have jurisdiction, the national government shall immediately take suitable measures, in accordance with its constitution and its laws, to the end that the competent authorities of the constituent units may adopt appropriate provisions for the fulfillment of this Convention.

3. Whenever two or more States Parties agree to form a federation or other type of association, they shall take care that the resulting federal Or other compact contains the provisions necessary for continuing and rendering effective the standards of this Convention in the new state that is organized.

Article 29. Restrictions Regarding Interpretation

No provision of this Convention shall be interpreted as:

(a) permitting any State Party, group, or person to suppress the enjoyment or exercise of the rights and freedoms recognized in this Convention or to restrict them to a greater extent than is provided for herein;

(b) restricting the enjoyment or exercise of any right or freedom recognized by virtue of the laws of any State Party or by virtue of another convention to which one of the said states is a party;

(c) precluding other rights or guarantees that are inherent in the human personality or derived from representative democracy as a form of government; or

(d) excluding or limiting the effect that the American Declaration of the Rights and Duties of Man and other international acts of the same nature may have.

Article 30. Scope of Restrictions

The restrictions that, pursuant to this Convention, may be placed on the enjoyment or exercise of the rights or freedoms recognized herein may not be applied except in accordance with laws enacted for reasons of general interest and in accordance with the purpose for which such restrictions have been established.

Article 31. Recognition of Other Rights

Other rights and freedoms recognized in accordance with the procedures established in Articles 76 and 77 May be included in the system of protection of this Convention.

CHAPTER V. RESPONSIBILITIES

Article 32. Relationship between Duties and Rights

1. Every person has responsibilities to his family, his community, and mankind.
2. The rights of each person are limited by the rights of others, by the security of all, and by the just demands of the general welfare, in a democratic society.

PART II. MEANS OF PROTECTION

CHAPTER VI. COMPETENT ORGANS

Article 33
The following organs shall have competence with respect to matters relating to the fulfillment of the commitments made by the States Parties to this Convention:

(a) the Inter-American Commission on Human Rights, referred to as "The Commission"; and
(b) the Inter-American Court of Human Rights, referred to as "The Court."

CHAPTER VII. INTER-AMERICAN COMMISSION ON HUMAN RIGHTS

SECTION 1. ORGANIZATION

Article 34
The Inter-American Commission on Human Rights shall be composed of seven members, who shall be persons of high moral character and recognized competence in the field of human rights.

Article 35
The Commission shall represent all the member countries of the Organization of American States.

Article 36
1. The members of the Commission shall be elected in a personal capacity by the General Assembly of the Organization from a list Of Candidates proposed by the governments of the member States.
2. Each of those governments may propose up to three candidates, who may be nationals of the states proposing them or of any other member state of the Organization of American States. When a slate of three is proposed, at least one of the candidates shall be a national of a state other than the one proposing the slate.

Article 37

1. The members of the Commission shall be elected for a term of four years and may be reelected only once, but the terms of three of the members chosen in the first election shall expire at the end of two years. Immediately following that election the General Assembly shall determine the names Of those three members by lot.
2. No two national of the same state may be members of the Commission.

Article 38

Vacancies that may occur on the Commission for reasons other than the normal expiration of a term shall be filled by the Permanent Council Organization in accordance with the provisions of the Statute of the Commission

Article 39

The Commission shall prepare its Statute, which it shall submit to the General Assembly for approval. It shall establish its own Regulations.

Article 40

Secretariat services for the Commission shall be furnished by the appropriate specialized unit of the General Secretariat of the Organization, This unit shall be provided with the resources required to accomplish the task assigned to it by the Commission.

SECTION 2. FUNCTIONS

Article 41

The main function of the Commission shall be to promote respect for and defense of human rights. In the exercise of its mandate, it shall have the following functions and powers:

(a) to develop an awareness of human rights among the peoples of America;

(b) to make recommendations to the governments of the member States, when it considers such action advisable, for the adoption of progressive measures in favor of human rights within the framework of their domestic law and constitutional provisions as well as appropriate measures to further the observance of those rights;

(c) to prepare such studies or reports as it considers advisable in the performance of its duties;

(d) to request the governments of the member states to supply it with information on the measures adopted by them in matters of human rights;

(e) to respond, through the General Secretariat of the Organization of American States, to inquiries made by the member states on matters related to human rights and, within the limits of its possibilities, to provide those states with the advisory services they request;

(f) to take action on petitions and other communications pursuant to its authority under the provisions of Articles 44 through 51 of this Convention; and

(g) to submit an annual report to the General Assembly of the Organization of American States.

Article 42

The States Parties shall transmit to the Commission a copy of each of the reports and studies that they submit annually to the Executive Committees of the Inter-American Economic and Social Council, and the Inter-American Council for Education, Science, and Culture, in their respective fields, so that the Commission May watch over the promotion of the fights implicit in the economic, social, educational, scientific, and cultural standards set forth in the Charter of the Organization of American States as amended by the Protocol of Buenos Aires.

Article 43

The States Parties undertake to provide the Commission with such information as it may request of them as to the manner in which their domestic law ensures the effective application of any provisions of this Convention

SECTION 3. COMPETENCE

Article 44

Any person or group of persons, or any non-governmental entity legally recognized in one or more member States of the Organization, may lodge Petitions with the Commission containing denunciations or complaints of violation of this Convention by a State Party.

Article 45

1. Any State Party may, when it deposits its instrument of ratification of adherence to this Convention, or at any later time, declare that it recognizes the competence of the Commission to receive and examine communications in which a State Party alleges that another State Party has committed a violation of a human right set forth in this Convention.

2. Communications presented by virtue of this article may be admitted and examined only if they are presented by a State Party that has made a declaration recognizing the aforementioned competence of the Commission. The Commission shall not admit any communication against a State Party that has not made such a declaration.

3. A declaration concerning recognition of competence may be made to be valid for an indefinite time, for a specified period, or for a specific case.

4. Declarations shall be deposited with the General Secretariat of the Organization of American States, which shall transmit copies thereof to the member states Of that Organization.

Article 46

1. Admission by the Commission of a petition or communication lodged in accordance with Articles 44 or 45 shall be subject to the following requirements:

    (a) that the remedies under domestic law have been pursued and exhausted in accordance with generally recognized principles of international law;

    (b) that the petition or communication is lodged within a period of six months from the date on which the party alleging violation of his rights was notified of the final judgment;

    (c) that the subject of the petition or communication is not pending in another international proceeding for settlement; and

(d) that, in the case of Article 44, the petition contains the name, nationality, profession, domicile, and signature of the person or persons or of the legal representative of the entity lodging the petition.

2. The provisions of paragraphs 1 (a) and 1 (b) of this article shall not be applicable when:

(a) the domestic legislation of the state concerned does not afford due process of law for the protection of the right or rights that live allegedly been violated:

(b) the party alleging violation of his rights has been denied access to the remedies under domestic law or has been prevented from exhausting them; or

(c) there has been unwarranted delay in rendering a final judgment under the aforementioned remedies.

Article 47

The Commission shall consider inadmissible any petition or communication submitted under Article 44 or 45 if:

(a) any or the requirements indicated in Article 46 has not been met;

(b) the petition or communication does not state facts that tend to establish a violation of the rights guaranteed by this Convention;

(c) the statements of the petitioner or of the state indicate that the petition or communication is manifestly groundless or obviously out of order; or

(d) the petition or communication is substantially tire same as one previously studied by the Commission or by another international organization.

SECTION 4. PROCEDURE

Article 48

1. When the Commission receives a petition or communication alleging violation of any of the rights protected by this Convention, it shall proceed as follows:

(a) If it considers the petition or communication admissible, it shall request information from the government of the state indicated as being responsible for the alleged violations and shall furnish that government a transcript of the pertinent portions of the petition or communication. This information shall be submitted within a reasonable period to be determined by the Commission in accordance with the circumstances of each case.

(b) After the information has been received, or after the period established has elapsed and the information has not been received, the Commission shall ascertain whether the grounds for the petition or communication still exist. If they do not, the Commission shall order the record to be closed.

(c) The Commission may also declare the petition or communication inadmissible or out of order on the basis of information or evidence subsequently received.

(d) If the record has not been closed, the Commission shall, with the knowledge of the parties, examine the matter set forth in the petition or communication in order to verify the facts. If necessary and advisable, the Commission shall carry out an investigation, for the effective conduct of which it shall request, and the states concerned shall furnish to it, all necessary facilities.

(e) The Commission may request the states concerned to furnish any pertinent information and, if so requested, shall hear oral statements or receive written statements from the parties concerned.

(f) The Commission shall place itself at the disposal of the parties concerned with a view to reaching a friendly settlement of the matter on the basis of respect for the human rights recognized in this Convention.

2. However, in serious and urgent cases, only the presentation of a petition or communication that fulfills all the formal requirements of admissibility shall be necessary in order for the Commission to conduct an investigation with the prior consent of the state in whose territory a violation has allegedly been committed.

Article 49

If a friendly settlement has been reached in accordance with paragraph 1(f) of Article 48, the Commission shall draw up a report, which shall be transmitted to the petitioner and to the States Parties to this Convention, and shall then be communicated to the Secretary General of the Organization of American States for publication. This report shall contain a brief statement of the facts and of the solution reached. If any party in the case so requests, the fullest possible information shall be provided to it.

Article 50

1. If a settlement is not reached, the Commission shall, within the time limit established by its Statute, draw up a report setting forth the facts and stating its conclusions. If the report, in whole or in part, does not represent the unanimous agreement of the members of the Commission, any member may attach to it a separate opinion. The written and oral statements made by the parties in accordance with paragraph 1 (e) of Article 48 shall also be attached to the report.
2. The report shall be transmitted to the states concerned, which shall not be at liberty to publish it.
3. In transmitting the report, the Committee may take such proposals and recommendations as it sees fit.

Article 51

1. If, within a period of three months from the date of the transmittal of the report of the Commission to the states concerned, the matter has not either been settle or submitted by the Commission or by the state concerned to the Court and its jurisdiction accepted, the Commission may, by the vote of an absolute majority of its members, set forth its opinion and conclusions concerning the question submitted for its consideration.
2. Where appropriate, the Commission shall make pertinent recommendation and shall prescribe a period within which the State is to take the measures that are incumbent upon it to remedy the situation examined.
3. When the prescribed period has expired, the Commission shall decide by the vote of an absolute majority of its members whether the state has taken adequate measures and whether to publish its report.

CHAPTER VIII. INTER-AMERICAN COURT OF HUMAN RIGHTS

SECTION 1. ORGANIZATION

Article 52

1. The Court shall consist of seven judges, national of the member states of the Organization, elected in an individual capacity from among jurists of the highest moral authority and of recognized competence in the field of human rights, who possess the qualifications required for the exercise of the highest judicial functions in conformity with the law of the state of which they are nationals or of the state proposes them as candidates.

2. No two judges may be nationals of the same state.

Article 53

1. The judges of the Court shall be elected by secret ballot by an absolute majority vote of the States Parties to the Convention, in the General Assembly of the Organization, from a panel of Candidates proposed by those states.
2. Each of the States Parties may propose up to three candidates, nationals of the State that proposes them or of any other member State of the Organization of American States. When a slate of three is proposed, at least one of the candidates shall be a national of a state other than the one proposing the slate.

Article 54

1. The judges of the Court shall be elected for a term of six years and may be reelected only once. The term of three of the judges chosen in the first election shall expire at the end of three years. Immediately after the election, the names of the three judges shall be determined by lot in the General Assembly.
2. A judge elected to replace a judge whose term has not expired shall complete the term of the latter.
3. The judge shall continue in office until the expiration of their term. However, they shall continue to serve with regard to cases that they have begun to hear and that are still pending, for which purposes they shall not be replaced by the newly elected judges.

Article 55

1. If a judge is a national of any of the States Parties to a Case submitted to the Court, he shall retain his right to hear that case.
2. If one of the judges called upon to hear a case should be a national of one of the States Parties to the case may appoint a person of its choice to serve on the Court as an *ad hoc* judge.
3. If among the judges called upon to hear a case none is a national of any of the States Parties to the case, each of the latter may appoint an *ad hoc* judge.
4. An *ad hoc* judge shall possess the qualifications indicated in Article 52.

5. If several States Parties to the Convention should have the same interest in a case, they shall be considered as a single party for purposes of the above provisions. In case of doubt, the Court shall decide.

Article 56
Five judges shall constitute a quorum for the transaction of business by the Court.

Article 57
The Commission shall appear in all cases before the Court.

Article 58
1. The Court shall have its seat at the place determined by the States parties to the Convention in the General Assembly of the Organization; however, it may convene in the territory of any member State of the Organization of American States when a majority of the Court consider it desirable, and with the prior consent of the state concerned. The seat of the Court may be changed by the States Parties to the Convention in the General Assembly by a two-thirds vote
2. The Court shall appoint its own Secretary.
3. The Secretary shall have his office at the place where the Court has its seat and shall attend the meetings that the Court may hold away from its seat.

Article 59
The Court shall establish its Secretariat, which shall function under the direction of the Secretary of the Court, in accordance with the administrative standards of the General Secretariat of the Organization in all respect not incompatible with the independence of the Court. The Staff of the Court's Secretariat shall be appointed by the Secretary General of the Organization, in consultation with the Secretary of the Court.

Article 60
The Court shall draw up its Statute which it shall submit to the General Assembly for approval. It shall adopt its own Rules of Procedure.

Section 2. Jurisdiction and Function

Article 61
1. Only the States Parties and the Commission shall have the right to submit a case to the Court.
2. In order for the Court to hear a case, it is necessary that the procedures set forth Articles 48 to 50 shall have been completed.

Article 62
1. A State party may, upon depositing its instrument of ratification or adherence to this Convention, or at any subsequent time, declare that it recognizes as binding, *ipso facto,* and not requiring special agreement, the jurisdiction of the Court on all matters relating to the interpretation or application of this Convention.
2. Such declaration may be made unconditionally on the condition of reciprocity, for a specified period, or for specific cases. It shall be presented to the Secretary General of the Organization. who shall transmit copies thereof to the other member states of the Organization and to the Secretary of the Court.
3. The jurisdiction of the Court shall comprise all cases concerning the interpretation and application of the provisions of this Convention that are submitted to it, provided that the States Parties to the case recognize or have recognized such jurisdiction, whether by special declaration pursuant to the preceding paragraphs or by a special agreement.

Article 63
1. If the Court finds that there has been a violation of a right or freedom protected by this Convention, the Court shall rule that the injured party be ensured the enjoyment of his right or freedom that was violated. It shall also rule, if appropriate, that the consequences of the measures or situation that constituted the breach of such right or freedom be remedied and that fair compensation be paid to the injured party.
2. In cases of extreme gravity and urgency, and when necessary to avoid irreparable damage to persons, the Court shall adopt such provisional measures as it deems pertinent in matters it has under consideration. With respect to a case not yet submitted to the Court may act at the request of the Commission.

Article 64
1. The member States of the Organization may consult the Court regarding the interpretation of this Convention or of other treaties concerning the protection of human rights in the American States. Within their spheres of competence, the organs listed in Charter of the Organization of American States, as amended by the Protocol of Buenos Aires,may in like manner consult the Court.
2. The Court, at the request of a member state of the Organization, may provide that state with opinions regarding the compatibility of any of its domestic laws with the aforesaid international instruments.

Article 65
To each regular session of the General Assembly of the Organization of American States the Court shall submit, for the Assembly's consideration, a report on its work during the previous year. It shall specify. in particular, the cases in which a state has not complied with its judgments, making any pertinent recommendations.

SECTION 3. PROCEDURE

Article 66
1. Reasons shall be given for the judgment of the Court.
2. If the judgment does not represent in whole or in part the unanimous opinion of the judges, any judge shall be entitled to have his dissenting or separate opinion attached to the judgment.

Article 67
The judgment of the Court shall be final and not subject to appeal. In case of disagreement as to the meaning or scope of the judgment, the Court shall interpret it at the request of any of the parties, provided the request is made within ninety days from the date of notification of the judgment.

Article 68
1. The States Parties to the Convention undertake to comply with the judgment of the Court in any case to which they are parties.
2. That part of a judgment that stipulates compensatory damages may be executed in the country concerned in accordance with domestic procedure governing the execution of judgments against the state.

Article 69

The parties to the case shall be notified of the judgment of the Court and it shall be transmitted to the States Parties to the Convention.

CHAPTER IX. COMMON PROVISIONS

Article 70

1. The judges of the Court and the members of the Commission shall enjoy, from the moment of their election and throughout their term of office, the immunities extended to diplomatic agents in accordance with international law. During the exercise of their official function they shall, in addition, enjoy the diplomatic privileges necessary for the performance of their duties.

2. At no time shall the judges of the Court or the members of the Commission be held liable for any decisions or opinions issued in the exercise of their functions.

Article 71

The position of judge of the Court or member of the Commission is incompatible with any other activity that might affect the independence or impartiality of such judge or member, as determined in the respective statutes.

Article 72

The judges of the Court and the members of the Commission shall receive emoluments and travel allowances in the form and under the conditions set forth in their statutes, with due regard for the importance and independence of their office. Such emoluments and travel allowances shall be determined in the budget of the Organization of American States, which shall also include the expenses of the Court and its Secretariat. To this end, the Court shall draw up its own budget and submit it for approval to the General Assembly through the General Secretariat. The latter May nor introduce any changes in it.

Article 73

The General Assembly may, only at the request of the Commission or the Court, as the case may be, determine sanctions to be applied against members of the Commission or judges of the Court when there are justifiable grounds for such action as set forth in the respective statutes. A vote of a two-thirds majority of the member states of the Organization shall be required for a decision in the case of members of the Commission and, in the case of judges of the Court, a two thirds majority vote of the States Parties to the Convention shall also be required.

PART III. GENERAL AND TRANSITORY PROVISIONS

CHAPTER X. SIGNATURE, RATIFICATION, RESERVATIONS, AMENDMENTS, PROTOCOLS, AND DENUNCIATION

Article 74
1. This Convention shall be open for signature and ratification by or adherence of any member state of the Organization of American States.
2. Ratification of or adherence to this Convention shall be made by the deposit of an instrument of ratification or adherence with the General Secretariat of the Organization of American States. As soon as eleven states have deposited their instruments of ratification or adherence, the Convention shall enter into force. With respect to any state that ratifies or adheres thereafter, the Convention enter into force on the date of the deposit of its instrument of ratification of adherence.
3. The Secretary General shall inform all member states of the Organization of the entry into force of the Convention.

Article 75
This Convention shall be subject to reservations only in conformity with tile provisions of the Vienna Convention on the Law of Treaties signed on May 23, 1969.

Article 76
1. Proposals to amend this Convention may be submitted to the General Assembly for the actions it deems appropriate by any State Party directly, and by the Commission or the Court through the Secretary General.
2. Amendments shall enter into force for the states ratifying them on the date when two-thirds of the States Parties to this Convention have deposited their respective instruments of ratification. With respect to the other

States Parties the, amendments shall enter into force on the dates on which they deposit their respective instruments of ratification.

Article 77

1. In accordance with Article 31, any State Party and the Commission may submit proposed protocol to this Convention for consideration by the States Parties at the General Assembly with a view to gradually including other rights and freedoms within its system of protection.
2. Each protocol shall determine the manner of its entry into force and shall be applied only among the States Parties to it.

Article 78

1. The States Parties may denounce this Convention at the expiration of a five-year period starting from the date of its entry into force and by means of notice given one year in advance. Notice of the denunciation shall be addressed to the Secretary General of the Organization, who shall inform the other States Parties.
2. Such a denunciation shall not have the effect of releasing the State Party concerned from the obligations contained in this Convention with respect to any act that may constitute a violation of those obligations and that has been taken by that state prior to the effective date of denunciation.

CHAPTER XI TRANSITORY PROVISIONS

SECTION I. INTER-AMERICAN COMMISSION ON HUMAN RIGHTS

Article 79

Upon entry into force of this Convention, the Secretary General shall in writing, request each member state of the Organization to present, within ninety days, its candidates for membership on the Inter-American Commission on Human Rights. The Secretary General shall prepare a list in alphabetical order of the candidates presented, and transmit it to the member states of the Organization at least thirty days prior to the next session of the General Assembly.

Article 80

The members of the Commission shall be elected by secret ballot of the General Assembly from the list of candidates referred to in Article 79. The candidates who obtain the largest number of votes and an absolute majority of the votes of the representatives of the member States shall be declared elected. Should it become necessary to have several ballots in order to elect all the members of the Commission, the candidates who receive the smallest votes shall be eliminated successively, in the manner determined by the General Assembly.

SECTION 2. INTER-AMERICAN COURT OF HUMAN RIGHTS

Article 81
Upon entry into force of this Convention, the Secretary General shall, in writing, request each State Party to present, within ninety days, its candidates for membership on the Inter-American Court of Human Rights. The Secretary General shall prepare a list in alphabetical order of candidates presented and transmit it to the States Parties at least thirty days prior to the next session of the General Assembly.

Article 82
The judges of the Court shall be elected from the list of candidates referred to in Article 81, by secret ballot of the States Parties to the Convention in the General Assembly.
The candidates who obtain the largest number of votes and an absolute majority of the votes of the representatives of the States Parties shall be declared elected. Should it become necessary to have several ballots in order to elect all the judges of the Court, the candidates who receive the smallest number of votes shall be eliminated successively, in the manner determined by the States Parties.

STATEMENTS AND RESERVATIONS

STATEMENT OF CHILE

The Delegation of Chile signs this Convention, subject to its subsequent parliamentary approval and ratification in accordance with the constitutional rules in force.

STATEMENT OF ECUADOR

The Delegation of Ecuador has the honor of signing the American Convention on Human Rights. It does not believe that it is necessary to make any specific reservation at this time, without prejudice to the general power set for the in the Convention itself that leaves the governments free to ratify it or not.

RESERVATION OF URUGUAY

Article 80.2 of the Constitution of Uruguay provides that citizenship is suspended for a person indicted according to law in a criminal prosecution that may result in a sentence of imprisonment in a penitentiary. This restriction on the exercise of the rights recognized in Article 23 of the Convention is not envisaged among the circumstances provided for in this respect by paragraph 2 of Article 23, for which reason the Delegation of Uruguay expresses a reservation on this matter. *In witness whereof,* the undersigned Plenipotentiaries, whose full powers were found in good and due form, sign this Convention, which shall be called "PACT ON SAN JOSE, COSTA RICA", (in the city of San Jose, Costa Rica, this twenty-second day of November, nineteen hundred and sixty-nine).

AFRICAN CHARTER ON HUMAN AND PEOPLES' RIGHTS[12]

PREAMBLE

The African States members of the Organization of African Unity, parties to the present convention entitled "African Charter on Human and Peoples' Rights".

---

[12] In force since 21 October 1987.

Recalling Decision 115(XVI)of the Assembly of Heads of State and Government a its Sixteenth Ordinary Session held in Monrovia, Liberia, from 17 to 20 July 1979 on the preparation of a "preliminary draft on an African Charter on Human and Peoples' Rights providing *inter alia* for the establishment of bodies to promote and protect human and peoples' rights";

Considering the Charter of the Organization of African Unity, which stipulates that "freedom, equality, justice and dignity are essential objectives for the achievement of the legitimate aspirations of the African peoples",

Reaffirming the pledge they solemnly made in Article 2 of the said charter to eradicate all forms of colonialism from Africa, to coordinate and intensify their cooperation and efforts to achieve a better life for the peoples of Africa and to promote international cooperation having due regard to the Charter of the United Nations and the Universal Declaration of Human Right;

Taking into consideration the virtues of their historical tradition and the values of African civilization which should inspire and characterize their reflection on the concept of human and peoples' rights;

Recognizing on the one hand, that fundamental human rights stem from the attributes of human beings, which justifies their national and international protection and on the other hand that the reality and respect of peoples rights should necessarily guarantee human rights;

Considering, that the enjoyment of rights and freedoms also implies the performance of duties on the part of everyone;

Convinced that it is henceforth essential to pay a particular attention to the right to development and that civil and political rights cannot be dissociated from economic, social and cultural rights in their conception as well as universality and that the satisfaction of economic, social and cultural rights is a guarantee for the enjoyment of civil and political rights;

Conscious of their duty to achieve the total liberation of Africa, the peoples of which are still struggling for their dignity and genuine independence, and undertaking to eliminate colonialism, neocolonialism, apartheid, Zionism and to dismantle aggressive foreign military bases and all forms of discrimination, particularly those based on race, ethnic group, color sex, language, religion or political opinions.

Reaffirming their adherence to the principles of human and peoples' rights and freedoms contained in the declarations, conventions and other instruments adopted by the Organization of African Unity, the Movement of Non-Aligned Countries and the United Nations.

Firmly convinced of their duty to promote and protect human and peoples' rights and freedoms taking into account the importance traditionally attached to these rights and freedoms in Africa;

Have agreed as follows:

PART I: RIGHTS AND DUTIES

CHAPTER I. HUMAN AND PEOPLES' RIGHTS

Article 1
The member States of the Organization of African Unity parties to the present Charter shall recognize the rights, duties and freedoms enshrined in this Charter and shall undertake to adopt legislative or other measures to give effect to them.

Article 2
Every individual shall be entitled to the enjoyment of the rights and freedoms recognized and guaranteed in the present Charter without distinction of any kind such as race, ethnic group, color, sex, language, religion, political or any other opinion, national and social origin, fortune, birth or other status.

Article 3
1. Every individual shall be equal before the law.
2. Every individual shall be entitled to equal protection of the law.

Article 4
Human beings are inviolable. Every human being shall be entitled to respect for his life and the integrity of his person. No one may be arbitrarily deprived of this right.

Article 5
Every individual shall have the right to the respect of the dignity inherent in a human being and to the recognition of his legal status. All forms of

exploitation and degradation of man particularly slavery, slave trade, torture, cruel, inhuman or degrading punishment and treatment shall be prohibited.

Article 6

Every individual shall have the right to liberty and to the security of his person. No one may be deprived of his freedom except for reasons and conditions previously laid down by law. In particular, no one may be arbitrarily arrested or detained.

Article 7

1. Every individual shall have the right to have his cause heard.
   This comprises:
   (a) the right to an appeal to competent national organs against acts of violating his fundamental rights as recognized and guaranteed by conventions, laws, regulations and customs in force;
   (b) the right to be presumed innocent until proved guilty by a competent court or tribunal;
   (c) the right to defence, including the right to be defended by counsel of his choice;
   (d) the right to be tried within a reasonable time by an impartial court or tribunal.
2. No one may be condemned for an act or omission which did not constitute a legally punishable offence at the time it was committed. No penalty may be inflicted for an offence for which no provision was made at the time it was committed. Punishment is personal and can be imposed only on the offender.

Article 8

Freedom of conscience, the profession and free practice of religion shall be guaranteed. No one may, Subject to law and order, be submitted to measures restricting the exercise of these freedoms.

Article 9

1. Every individual shall have the right to receive information.
2. Every individual shall have the right to express and disseminate his opinions within the law.

Article 10

1. Every individual shall have the right to free association provided that he abides by the law.
2. Subject to the obligation of solidarity provided for in Article 29 no   one may be compelled to join an association.

Article 11

Every individual shall have the right to assemble freely with   others. The exercise of this right shall be subject only to necessary restrictions provided for by law in particular those enacted in the interest of national security, the safety, health, ethics and rights and freedoms of others.

Article 12

1. Every individual shall have the right to freedom of movement and residence within the borders of a State provided he abides by the law.
2. Every individual shall have the right to leave any country including his own and to return to his country. This right may only be subject to restriction, provided for by law for the protection of national security, law and order, public health or morality.
3. Every individual shall have the right, when persecuted, to seek and obtain asylum in other countries in accordance with laws of those countries and international conventions.
4. A non-national legally admitted in a territory of a State party to the present Charter, may only be expelled from it by virtue of a decision taken in accordance with the law.
5. The mass expulsion of non-national shall be prohibited. Mass expulsion shall be that which is aimed at national, racial, ethnic or religious groups.

Article 13

1. Every citizen shall have the right to participate freely in the government of his country, either directly or through freely chosen representatives in accordance with the provisions of the law.
2. Every citizen shall have the right of equal access to the public service of his country.
3. Every individual shall have the right of access to public property and services in strict equality of all persons before the law.

Article 14
The right to property shall be guaranteed. It may only be encroached upon in the interest of public need or in the general interest of the community and in accordance with the provisions of appropriate laws.

Article 15
Every individual shall have the right to work under equitable and satisfactory conditions, and shall receive equal pay for equal work.

Article 16
1. Every individual shall have the right to enjoy the best attainable state of physical and mental health.
2. States parties to the present Charter shall take the necessary measures to protect the health of their people and to ensure that they receive medical attention when they are nick.

Article 17
1. Every individual shall have the right to education.
2. Every individual may freely, take part in the cultural life of
his community.
3. The promotion and protection of morals and traditional values recognized by the community shall be the duty of the State.

Article 18
1. The family shall be the natural unit and basis of society. It shall be protected by the State which shall take care of its physical health and moral.
2. The State shall have the duty to assist the family which is the custodian of morals and traditional values recognized by the community.
3. The State shall ensure the elimination of every discrimination against women and also censure the protection of the rights of the woman and the child as stipulated in international declarations and conventions.
4. The aged and the disabled shall also have the right to special measures of protection in keeping with their physical or moral needs.

Article 19
All peoples shall be equal; they shall enjoy the same respect and shall have the same rights. Nothing shall justify the domination of a people by another.

Article 20

1. All peoples shall have the right to existence. They shall have the unquestionable and inalienable right to self-determination. They shall freely determine their political status and shall pursue their economic and social development according to the policy they have freely chosen.
2. Colonized or oppressed peoples shall have the right to free themselves from the bonds of domination by resorting to any means recognized by the international community.
3. All peoples shall have the right to the assistance of the States parties to the present Charter in their liberation struggle against foreign domination, be it political, economic or cultural.

Article 21

1. All peoples shall freely dispose of their wealth and natural resources. This right shall be exercised in the exclusive interest of the people. In no case shall a peoples be deprived of it.
2. In case of spoliation the dispossessed people shall have the right to the lawful recovery of its property as well as to an adequate compensation.
3. The free disposal of wealth and natural resources shall be exercised without prejudice to the obligation of promoting international economic cooperation based on mutual respect, equitable exchange and the principles of international law.
4. States parties to the present Charter shall individually and collectively exercise the right to free disposal of their wealth and natural resources with a view to strengthening African unity and solidarity.
5. States parties to the present Charter shall undertake to eliminate all forms of foreign economic exploitation particularly that practiced by international monopolies so as to enable their peoples to fully benefit from the advantages derived from national resources.

Article 22

1. All peoples shall have the right to their economic, social and cultural development with due regard to their freedom and identity and in the equal enjoyment of the common heritage of mankind.
2. States shall have the duty, individually or collectively, to ensure the exercise of the right to development.

Article 23

1. All peoples shall have the right to national and international peace and security. The principles of solidarity and friendly relations implicitly affirmed by the Charter of the United Nations and reaffirmed by that of the Organization of African Unity shall govern relations between States.
2. For the purpose of strengthening peace, solidarity and friendly relations, States parties to the present Charter shall ensure that:
   (a) any individual enjoying the right of asylum under 12 of the present Charter shall not engage in subversive activities against the country of origin or any other State party to the present Charter;
   (b) their territories shall not be used as bases for subversive or terrorist activities against the people of any other State party to the present Charter.

Article 24

All peoples shall have the right to a general satisfactory environment favorable to their development.

Article 25

States parties to the present Charter shall have the duty to promote and ensure through teaching, education and publication, the respect of the rights and freedoms contained in the present Charter and to see to it that these freedoms and rights as well as corresponding obligations and duties are understood.

Article 26

States Parties to the present Charter shall have the duty to guarantee the independence of the Courts and shall allow the establishment and improvement of appropriate national institutions entrusted with the promotion and protection of the rights and freedoms guaranteed by the present Charter.

CHAPTER II. DUTIES

Article 27

1. Every individual shall have duties towards his family and society, the State and other legally recognized communities and the international community.

2. The rights and freedoms of each individual shall be exercised with due regard to the rights of others, collective security, morality and common interest.

Article 28

Every individual shall have the duty to respect and consider his fellow beings without discrimination, and to maintain relations aimed at promoting, safeguarding and reinforcing mutual respect and tolerance.

Article 29

The individual shall also have the duty:

1. To preserve the harmonious development of the family and to work for the cohesion and respect of the family; to respect his parents at all times, to maintain them in case of need;
2. To serve his national community by placing his physical and intellectual abilities at its service;
3. Not to compromise the security of the State whose national or resident he is;
4. To preserve and strengthen social and national solidarity, particularly when the latter is threatened;
5. To Preserve and strengthen the national independence and the territorial integrity of his country and to contribute to its defence in accordance with the law;
6. To work to the best of his abilities and competence, and to pay taxes imposed by law in the interest of the society;
7. To preserve and strengthen positive African cultural values in his relations with other members of the society, in the spirit of tolerance, dialogue consultation and, in general, to contribute to the promotion of the moral well being of society;
8. To contribute to the best of his abilities, at all times and at all levels, to the promotion and achievement of African unity.

PART II. MEASURES OF SAFEGUARD

CHAPTER I. ESTABLISHMENT AND ORGANIZATION OF THE AFRICAN COMMISSION ON HUMAN AND PEOPLES' RIGHTS

Article 30

An African Commission on Human and Peoples' Rights, hereinafter called "the Commission", shall be established within the Organization of African Unity to promote human and peoples' rights and ensure their protection in Africa.

Article 31

1. The Commission shall consist of eleven members chosen from amongst African personalities of the highest reputation, known for their high morality, integrity, impartiality and competence in matters of humans and peoples' rights; particular consideration being given to persons having legal experience.
2. The members of the Commission shall serve in their personal capacity.

Article 32

The Commission shall not include more than one national of the same State.

Article 33

The members of the Commission shall be elected by secret ballot by the Assembly of Heads of State and Government, from a list of persons nominated by the States parties to the present Charter.

Article 34

Each State party to the present Charter may not nominate more than two candidates. The candidates must have the nationality of one of the States parties to the present Charter. When two candidates are nominated by a State, one of them may not be a national of that State.

Article 35

1. The Secretary General of the Organization of African Unity shall invite States parties to the present Charter at least four months before the elections to nominate candidates:

2. The Secretary General of Organization of African Unity shall make an alphabetical list of the persons thus nominated and communicate it to the Heads of State and Government at least one month before the elections.

Article 36
The members of the Commission shall be elected for a six year period and shall be eligible for re-election. However, the term of office of four of the members elected at the first election shall terminate after two years and the term of office of the three others, at the end of the four years.

Article 37
Immediately after the first election, the Chairman of the Assembly of Heads of State and Government of the Organization of African Unity shall draw lots to decide the names of those referred to in Article 26.

Article 38
After their election, the members of the Commission shall make a solemn declaration to discharge their duties impartially and faithfully.

Article 39
1. In case of death or resignation of a member of the Commission, Chairman of the Commission shall immediately inform the Secretary General of the Organization of African Unity, who shall declare the seat vacant from the date of death or from the date on which the resignation takes effect.
2. If, in the unanimous opinion of other members of the Commission, a member has stopped discharging his duties for any reason other than a temporary absence, the Chairman of the Commission shall inform the Secretary General of the Organization of African Unity, who shall then declare the seat vacant.
3. In each of the cases anticipated above, the Assembly of Heads of State and Government shall replace the member whose seat became vacant for the remaining period of his term unless the period is less than six months.

Article 40
Every member of the Commission shall be in office until the date his successor assumes office.

Article 41
The Secretary General of the Organization of African Unity appoint the Secretary of the Commission. He shall also provide the staff and services necessary for the effective discharge of the duties of the Commission. The Organization of African Unity shall bear the costs of the staff and services.

Article 42
1. The Commission shall elect its Chairman and Vice Chairman for a two year period. They shall be eligible for re-election.
2. The Commission shall lay down its rules of procedure.
3. Seven members shall form a quorum.
4. In case of an equality of votes, the Chairman shall have a casting vote.
5. The Secretary General may attend the meetings of the Commission. He shall neither participate in deliberations nor shall he be entitled to vote. The Chairman of the Commission may, however, invite him to speak.

Article 43
In discharging their duties, members of the Commission shall enjoy diplomatic privileges and immunities provided for in the General Convention in the Privileges and Immunities of the Organization of African Unity.

Article 44
Provision shall be made for the emoluments and allowances of the members of the Commission in the Regular Budget of the Organization of African Unity.

CHAPTER II. MANDATE OF THE COMMISSION

Article 45
The functions of the Commission shall be:
1. To promote Human and Peoples' Rights and in particular:
   (a) to collect documents undertake studies and researches on African problems in the field of human and peoples' rights, organize seminars, symposia and conferences, disseminate information, encourage national and local institutions concerned with human and peoples' rights, and should the case arise, give its views or make recommendations to Governments.

(b) to formulate and lay down, principles and rules aimed at solving legal problems relating to human and peoples' rights and fundamental freedoms upon which African Governments may base their legislations.

(c) cooperate with other African and international institutions concerned with the promotion and protection of human and peoples' rights.

2. Ensure the protection of human and peoples' rights under conditions laid down in the present Charter.

3. Interpret all the provisions of the present Charter at the request of a State party, an institution of the OAU or an African Organization recognized by the OAU.

4. Perform any other tasks which may be entrusted to it by the Assembly of Heads of State and Government.

CHAPTER III. PROCEDURE OF THE COMMISSION

Article 46

The Commission may resort to any appropriate method of investigation; it may hear from the Secretary General of the Organization of African Unity or any other person capable of enlightening it.

Communication from States

Article 47

If a State party to the present Charter has good reasons to believe that another State party to this Charter has violated the provisions of the Charter, it may draw, by written communication, the attention of the State to the matter. This communication shall also be addressed to the Secretary General of the OAU and to the Chairman of the Commission. Within three months of the receipt of the communication, the State to which the communication is addressed shall give the inquiring State, written explanation or statement elucidating the matter. This should include as much as possible relevant information relating to the laws and rules of procedure applied and applicable, and the redress already given or course of action available.

Article 48

If within three months from the date on which the original communication is received by the State to which it is addressed, the issue is not settled to the satisfaction of the two States involved through bilateral negotiation or by any

other peaceful procedure, either State shall have the right to submit the matter
to the Commission through the Chairman and shall notify the other States
involved.

Article 49
Notwithstanding the provisions of Article 47, if a State party to the present
Charter considers that another State party has violated the provisions of the
Charter, it may refer the matter directly to the Commission by addressing a
communication to the Chairman, to the Secretary General of the Organization
of African Unity and the State concerned.

Article 50
The Commission can only deal with a matter submitted to it after making sure
that all local remedies, if they exist, have been exhausted, unless it is obvious
to the Commission that the procedure of achieving these remedies would be
unduly prolonged.

Article 51
1. The Commission may ask the States concerned to provide it with all
   relevant information.
2. When the Commission is considering the matter, States concerned may be
   represented before it and submit written or oral representation.

Article 52
After having obtained from the States concerned and from other sources all
the information it deems necessary and after having tried all appropriate
means to reach an amicable solution based on the respect of Human and
Peoples' Rights, the Commission shall prepare, within a reasonable period of
time from the notification referred to in Article 48, a report Stating the facts
and its findings. This report shall be sent to the States concerned and
communicated to the Assembly of Heads of State and Government.

Article 53
While transmitting its report, the Commission may make to the Assembly of
Heads of State and Government such recommendations as it deems useful.

Article 54

The Commission shall submit to each ordinary Session of the Assembly of Heads of State and Government a report on its activities.

Other Communications

Article 55

1. Before each Session, the Secretary of the Commission shall make a list of the communications other than those of States parties to the present Charter and transmit them to the members of the Commission, who shall indicate which communications should be considered by the Commission.
2. A communication shall be considered by the Commission if a simple majority of its members so decide.

Article 56

Communications relating to human and peoples' rights referred to in Article 55 received by the Commission, shall be considered if they:

1. Indicate their authors even if the latter request anonymity,
2. Are compatible with the Charter of the Organization of African Unity or with the present Charter,
3. Are not written in disparaging or insulting language directed against the State concerned and its institutions or to the Organization of African Unity,
4. Are not based exclusively on news discriminated through the mass media,
5. Are sent after exhausting local remedies, if any, unless it is obvious that this procedure is unduly prolong,
6. Are submitted within a reasonable period from the time local remedies are exhausted or from the date the Commission is seized of the matter and
7. Do not deal with cases which have been settled by these States involved in accordance with the principles of the Charter of the United Nations, or the Charter of the Organization of African Unity or the provisions of the present Charter.

Article 57

Prior to any substantive consideration, all communication shall be brought to the knowledge of the State concerned by the Chairman of the Commission.

Article 58

1. When it appears after deliberations of the Commission that one or more communications apparently relate to special cases which reveal the existence of a series of serious or massive violations of human and peoples' rights, the Commission shall draw the attention of the Assembly of Heads of State and Government to these special cases.
2. The Assembly of Heads of State and Government may then request the Commission to undertake an in-depth study of these cases and make a factual report, accompanied by its findings and recommendations.
3. A case of emergency duly noticed by the Commission shall be submitted by the latter to the Chairman of the Assembly of Heads of State and Government who may request an in-depth study.

Article 59

1. All measures taken within the provisions of the present Chapter shall remain confidential until such a time as the Assembly of the Heads of State and Government shall otherwise decide.
2. However, the report shall be published by the Chairman of the Commission upon the decision of the Assembly of Heads of State and Government.
3. The report on the activities of the Commission shall be published by its Chairman after it has been considered by the Assembly of Heads of State and Government.

CHAPTER IV: APPLICABLE PRINCIPLES

Article 60

The Commission shall draw inspiration from international law on human and peoples' rights, particularly from the provisions of various African instruments on human and peoples' rights, the Charter of the United Nations, the Charter of the Organization of African Unity, the Universal Declaration of Human Rights, other instruments adopted by the United Nations and by African Countries in the field of human and peoples' rights as well as from the provisions of various instruments adopted within the Specialized Agencies of the United Nations of which the parties to the present Charter are members.

Article 61

The Commission shall also take into consideration, as subsidiary measures to determine the principles of law, other general or special international conventions, laying down rules expressly recognized by member states of the Organization of African Unity, African practices consistent with international norms on human and peoples' rights, customs generally accepted as laws, general principles of law recognized by African States as well as legal precedents and doctrine.

Article 62

Each state party shall undertake to submit every two years, from the date the present Charter comes into force, a report on legislative or other measures taken with a view to giving effect to the rights and freedoms recognized and guaranteed by the present Charter.

Article 63

1. The present Charter shall be open to signature, ratification or adherence of the member state of the Organization of African Unity.
2. The instruments of ratification or adherence to the present Charter shall be deposited with the Secretary general of the Organization of African Unity.
3. The present Charter shall come into force three months after the reception by the Secretary General of the instruments of ratification or adherence of a simple majority of the members states of the Organization of African Unity.

PART III. GENERAL PROVISIONS

Article 64

1. After the coming into force of the present Charter, members of the Commission shall be elected in accordance with the relevant Articles of the present Charter
2. The Secretary General of the Organization of African Unity shall convene the first meeting of the Commission at the Headquarters of the Organization within three months of the constitution of the Commission. Thereafter, the Commission shall be convened by its Chairman whenever necessary but at least once a year.

Article 65
For each of the States that will ratify or adhere to the present Charter after its coming into force, the Charter shall take effect three months after the date of the deposit by that State of its instruments of ratification or adherence.

Article 66
Special protocols and agreements may, if necessary, supplement the provisions of the present Charter.

Article 67
The Secretary General of the Organization of African Unity shall inform member states of the Organization of the deposit of each instrument of ratification or adherence.

Article 68
The present Charter may be amended if a State party makes a written request to that effect to the Secretary General of the Organization of African Unity. The Assembly of Heads of State and Government may only consider the draft amendment after all the States parties have been duly informed of it and the Commission has given its opinion on it at the request of the sponsoring State. The amendment shall be approved by a simple majority of the State parties. It shall come into force for each State which has accepted it in accordance with its constitutional procedure three months after the Secretary General has received notice of the acceptance.

Adopted by the eighteenth Assembly of Heads of State and Government- June 1991, Nairobi, Kenya.

INDEX